Emerson and New Thought

"In my opinion, *Emerson and New Thought* is a must read, especially for those desiring an enhanced way of experiencing this human journey.

"Author Carol Carnes has enhanced the awareness of many with her exquisite ability to convey spiritual truth that may be elusive to the seeker. It has been my blessing to experience her writing brilliance for many years.

"*Emerson and New Thought* will open the consciousness of those who may have put Ralph Waldo Emerson's writings aside, finding difficulty in understanding his magnificent esoteric writings. For others, including newcomers seeking guidance from this gifted philosopher, an open door to awakening will be facilitated."

—Rev. Dr. Angelo Pizelo
   Founding President, Emerson Theological Institute

"I think the publishers got it right when they invited Dr. Carol Carnes to write a commentary on Emerson's essays and how they influenced the Science of Mind/New Thought movement. Why? Because Carol Carnes in her heart of hearts is not only a Transcendentalist but also a wonderfully gifted teacher. And like all great teachers, she embodies her subject.

"*Emerson and New Thought* brings to modern life the depth and meaning behind Emerson's wonderful works. It is fresh, vibrant, and soul-stirring, not only for students of metaphysics but for everyone and anyone who seeks awareness of the beauty and goodness of life. Without hesitation, I'm recommending it as a must-read!"

—Rev. Dr. Kenn Gordon
   Former President, International Centers
   for Spiritual Living

"When Carol Carnes comes together with Ralph Waldo Emerson, veils lift and clarity shines through. Timeless truths shared in a contemporary way bring depth and insight to the classic essays. Let the lights come on for you as you return to some of Emerson's finest work brought to life by Carnes' creative and heartfelt reflections."

—Rev. Dr. David Leonard
    Spiritual Director, Huntsville Alabama
    Center for Spiritual Living

"When it comes to teaching the Science of Mind, Carol Carnes is long known for her skillful interpretations and commitment to her subject. She applies her understanding of Holmes' principles to her intellectual pursuits, informing her life choices and extending to us in this current work a worldview that includes the brilliant innate insights of Emerson. Carnes is a serious teacher for serious students of these teachings, a characterization well supported by a lifetime of dedication to this path."

—Dr. Barbara Fields
    Executive Director, Association for
    Global New Thought

"Carol Carnes not only sees into the minds of great metaphysicians; she also knows the minds of her readers. I've lost count of the number of times she has addressed exactly the topic or problem I'm facing in life. Her clarity shines like a light that uplifts and creates an even higher level of understanding, which is much appreciated."

—Dr. Bill Little
    Spiritual Director, Center of Spiritual Awakening
    Pacific Grove, CA

Reading Emerson is like drinking water to me.

—Ernest Holmes

Emerson
and
New Thought

HOW EMERSON'S ESSAYS INFLUENCED
THE SCIENCE OF MIND PHILOSOPHY

RALPH WALDO EMERSON
WITH COMMENTARY BY
DR. CAROL CARNES

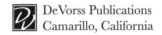
DeVorss Publications
Camarillo, California

EMERSON AND NEW THOUGHT
Copyright © 2021
by Carol Carnes

Print ISBN: 9780875169231
ebook ISBN: 9780875169248

Library of Congress Catalog Card Number: 2021942175
First Printing, 2021

Selected chapters from Emerson's Essays by
Ralph Waldo Emerson were originally published in 1926
by Thomas Y. Crowell Company, Inc.

DeVorss & Company, Publisher
P.O. Box 1389
Camarillo CA 93011-1389
www.devorss.com

Printed in the United States of America

Table of Contents

Acknowledgments

Thank you to Gary Peattie of DeVorss Publications. He asked if I might be interested in writing commentary on the main essays used in teaching Ralph Waldo Emerson, especially relating them to Ernest Holmes' Science of Mind. I hesitated, not sure if I was the right person for the job. It was his commitment to creating a New Thought user-friendly edition of Emerson's Essays that convinced me to get on board.

I was greatly encouraged by Dr. David Leonard, my dear friend and colleague and occasional dancing partner, who is somewhat of an Emerson scholar. Thank you for the push from behind, David.

Thank you to my daughter Maggie, who insisted that I accept the offer and who encouraged me during the writing process. There is nothing quite like a cheerleader who thinks you are a winner!

To Emerson himself. When I first began my studies in New Thought, I attended a workshop. We went into quiet time and were asked to bring up an image of a "guide." I saw a nice-looking man whom I did not recognize. Some time later I picked up the Emerson book of essays and there was my "guide," Emerson! I had never read him nor seen a picture of him. He has been my "go-to guy" (if not guide) ever since.

Dedication

To the thousands of students who have given their time and treasure to the study of New Thought.

To those teachers and ministers who have presented Emerson's writings as important contributions to the Science of Mind.

To my teachers, in particular Dr. Bill Little, who brought East and West, science and spirituality, into every class, every conversation, every Sunday lesson. He is very Emersonian.

Foreword

Generations of Americans have been influenced by the writings of Ralph Waldo Emerson, perhaps unknowingly. He is the most often quoted American, second only to Abraham Lincoln. Some of our favorite terms to live by are his. "Hitch Your Wagon to a Star" is but one example. Emerson had a profoundly witty and insightful writing style that, oddly, some students find hard to follow. Poetic and lyrical at times, often his words are stinging barbs, aimed at the bigot, the pompous, the ignorant. His influence on Dr. Ernest Holmes, author of the Science of Mind and founder of the spiritual teaching by the same name, was immediate. Holmes credits Emerson with giving him the more mystical view of the Divinity within all sentient life, indeed all life, dispelling the earlier metaphysical notion that Spirit and matter were separate. That is a major distinction between Christian Science and Science of Mind.

Teachers of the Science of Mind are expected to be more than a little familiar with Emerson's essays, which are part of their training and required reading. Having said that, Emerson is not every minister's cup of tea. Some find the language old fashioned, stilted, or flowery. Not so with Dr. Carol Carnes. She has said that the first time she read "Self-Reliance," sitting on a beach in Hawaii, she found herself laughing out loud at his turns of phrase and his wry sense of humor, not to mention the stunning clarity of his observations on human behavior. Her love of Emerson has infused her writings, her classroom lessons, and her daily blog, "Living Consciously." Dr. Carnes' ability to "translate" Emerson into modern language and show the relevance to our lives today is one reason her students have said, "I never understood him until I took this class."

Emerson and New Thought provides readers with insight that sheds new light on the course material presented by Centers for Spiritual Living. This presentation of five of Emerson's most beloved essays has been edited to be "gender inclusive." While it was common in his day to refer to humanity as "mankind" and to people in general as "man," that can be difficult for many to embrace today. The writing itself has not been changed except for a very few places where additional editing was needed for today's reader.

Dr. Carnes interprets, comments, and invites us to discover our own personal application of these timeless writings. Anyone reading the five essays, "Self-Reliance," "Spiritual Law," "Circles," "Compensation," and "The Over-Soul," will benefit from her guidance. Emerson earned his place in the pantheon of the world's greatest minds—past, present, and possibly future.

Enjoy!

What lies behind you and what lies in front of you

pales in comparison to what lies inside of you.

—Ralph Waldo Emerson

Self-Reliance
Emerson the Humorist

Overview:

IN THIS ESSAY EMERSON PULLS NO PUNCHES.
HE MAINTAINS THAT TO BE GREAT IS TO BE
MISUNDERSTOOD, THAT SOCIETY ATTEMPTS TO
ROB US OF OUR PERSONAL AUTHORITY. HIS WIT
SHINES THROUGH, BUT HE IS DEADLY SERIOUS.

I**T IS A RARE GIFT** to be wildly funny while dispensing timeless Truth. Witty and wise, sometimes hilarious in his observations of human behavior, Ralph Waldo Emerson could not hide his spiritual Heart behind his scathing humor. He wrote in his journal: "I like man, but not men." He loved humanity, but individuals with their arrogance and pomp disappointed and irritated him, although he granted them the possibility of realizing a greater Self.

Emerson's essay "Self-Reliance" may be one of the most important pieces of written advice ever to be published. He admonished us to remain ourselves, not

1

shaped and molded by outer events or the opinions of others. His stance was not one of standing up against anything, rather to sit with the Self and rely on what is within. Whereas Marcus Aurelius made good sense of stoicism, implying a kind of protection against the ignorance that was present in everyday life, Emerson was all about the presence of perfection, the kernel of genius in human life, the Divine in all sentient Beings. He knew a fool or arrogance when he saw it, yet he claimed there was present a better person than what was being expressed. That is a generosity that is rare in any age. It reminds us of the teachings of Jesus. Love thy neighbor as thyself. In other words, acknowledge the perfection within, the dormant genius.

To trust one's own thoughts is the overriding message of this essay. In some way we are one with the originating Intelligence, able to draw from it (our genius) and to follow its guidance (intuition). "Self-Reliance" appealed to Ernest Holmes for its insistence on our innate genius, insisting that his "Science of Mind" did not arise in a vacuum, but was greatly influenced by the brilliance of Emerson, the logic of Thomas Troward, the mysticism of the Eastern teachings, including the revelations of science, philosophy, and psychology. Emerson can be heard throughout the teachings of Holmes. While not one hundred percent identical, there is a natural commingling of the two. One feels these two men were spiritual brothers.

Emerson's witty references to his son being bashful and silent around his parents, doing nothing more than eating, but able to roll out like "bell strokes" words of wisdom to his peers, is the stuff of a stand-up comic. (Emerson could have been the George Carlin of his day had he chosen a career on the stage!) The difference between Emerson and others who call out the injustices and the stupidity of humanity is that Emerson never gave up on us. He felt that within were the makings of a superior Being, if we would but realize it. The message of Holmes is very similar. Holmes also was no fool and called it as he saw it, but he never condemned or denounced the one who seemed lost. His faith in humanity was unassailable. He created the Science of Mind to awaken the student to the deeper self, the greater possibility inherent within them.

Holmes would say it like this: "God is the power that makes all things new. It knows nothing of the past, only the ever present now. It does not heal or repair. It makes new all things right now." Therefore, a prayer to ask God to fix a problem lacks power. Emerson wrote: "Prayer is the contemplation of the facts of life from the highest point of view. It is the soliloquy of a beholding and jubilant soul."

Emerson seems to know human nature well when he reminds us how often we have had a great insight or idea, done nothing with it, only to see it masterfully on display by someone else. We feel cheated somehow, but, in fact, our lack of self-reliance inhibited our expression of it. "Who me? How could I do that?" We tend to stop there. A good affirmation is: "I can do this. I know how. I have the time."

Holmes designed Spiritual Mind Treatment (scientific prayer) along those lines. We behold the Truth of wholeness and infinite possibility, regardless of the current "facts" of our life. We take our beholding to a level that causes us to feel a surge of well-being, a sense that "it is so now." In fact, Holmes would have us "turn entirely away from the condition" and enter the spiritual realm of wholeness, where there is no such thing as disease or lack. Emerson said something similar: that we should "sit at home with Cause."

The entire essay is a kind of offering to the reader. Emerson is trying to bring us into a realization of how powerful we are; how loved by the conscious universe and how this now moment is where that power and love can be felt and actualized. He makes quite a point of showing how we have lost our edge, as it were. "The civilized man has built a coach but has lost the use of his feet." Emerson felt that adopted customs and modern conveniences could rob us of our native intelligence. His advice was about balance. Not to vilify modernity, but to keep our feet on the ground and our head in the spiritual. One informs the other. Holmes taught something of that nature. He said we need our intellect but tell it to lay an egg and it will fail. "Now, he quipped, how will you get a chicken?" He wanted us to use our intellect to access the finer realms of mind, beyond and behind the ego. To Holmes and Emerson, Intuition is the spark of the Divine in us. It is beyond the intellect but informs it. It comes through the one who has placed their trust in it. How can we trust what we have not known? How can we hear the Infinite within if our entire attention is on the outer world?

We need our intellect to ponder new ideas, but we also need our intuition to feel the truth of them. That takes practice. Nature is a great aide in reminding us of the perfection and beauty of this universe. We want to get our hands in the dirt, plant things, hear the birdsong, smell the flowers, talk to the trees. It is imperative that to be in the world but not of it, we need to be in both realities at once. Emerson lived on the edge of the woods where he spent much time, balancing his intellectual prowess with the simplicity of Nature. He relished the call of the wild, so to speak.

Holmes said the gardener sees the Divine in his fields, the mother in the eyes of her newborn. Both of these brilliant thinkers were Mystics as well as intellectual giants. Think about the stories of Jesus; was this not true of him as well? He was able to convey deep spiritual truth through parables. Many of them were references to seeds and soil. He spoke Truth to Power. His revelations came from within, His mystical mind perceived a Reality beyond what humanity was experiencing in his part of the world. Like Holmes and Emerson, his message was, "There is a power in this universe, greater than you, and you can use it."

Although Emerson was born in Britain, he spent almost his entire life in America. He ridiculed the aspects of American life that preferred everything European. He felt travel was a waste of time if for any other reason than study or to learn more about oneself. It was an extension of his comments on how we give up our self for the opinions of others too easily. He wanted us to claim our real self and to rely on it.

Be "like a boy assured of a good dinner," was Emerson's spiritual advice. A child living in a comfortable home with loving parents is not spoiled, because he expects "a good dinner" or knows his college tuition will be paid, or that his parents will always support him. He is assured of his supply of love, support, money, and care. That is the relationship Emerson felt we ought to have with our Source (God). We ought to be cheerfully expectant of our Good. Of course, we must partici- pate in its coming to fruition. There is a strong message deeply rooted in our Source, and each one of us has the abililty to cultivate a relationship with that Genius within.

Holmes taught us to respect our Source, for it was the origin of everything. He reminded us that no one knows why, for example, blue and yellow together make green, but that they do, and we can use green however we might desire. It was his practicality that made his teaching so accessible. Emerson framed his advice in poetic flourishes, yet if the student takes time to break down his more flowery writing, there will be seen a practical use for the sentiment. He was about helping humanity reach a higher level of living. That is exactly what Holmes intended as well.

At the core of this essay, Emerson is telling us to trust the Laws that govern the universe. "Do not believe good is happening because of a political victory, a rise of rents, the recovery of your sick or the return of your absent friend, or that some other quire external event raises your spirit. You think good days are preparing for you. Do not believe it. It can never be so. Nothing can bring you peace but yourself. Nothing can bring you peace but the triumph of principles."

"This is a spiritual universe, governed by spiritual laws," said Holmes. Can we see how that frees us from relying on luck and the generosity of others, or perhaps the stock market or the weather? Only our Self-Awareness in accord with nature, announcing its wholeness and its cheerful expectation to be granted the content of its mind, will prove to be the real Cause of our Good. These Laws are Love in action. That is Self-Reliance.

—Dr. Carol Carnes

Self-Reliance

Ralph Waldo Emerson

"Man is his own star; and the soul that can render
an honest and a perfect man, commands all light,
all influence, all fate; nothing to him falls early or
too late. Our acts our angels are, or good or ill,
our fatal shadows that walk by us still."

—*Epilogue to Beaumont and Fletcher's*
Honest Man's Fortune.

Cast the bantling on the rocks,
Suckle him with the she-wolf's teat;

Wintered with the hawk and fox,
Power and speed be hands and feet.

I READ THE OTHER DAY some verses written by an eminent painter which were original and not conventional. Always the soul hears an admonition in such
lines, let the subject be what it may. The sentiment they
instill is of more value than any thought they may contain. To believe your own thought, to believe that what
is true for you in your private heart is true for all—that
is genius. Speak your latent conviction, and it shall be

the universal sense; for always the inmost becomes the outmost—and our first thought is rendered back to us by the trumpets of the Last Judgment. Familiar as the voice of the mind is to each, the highest merit we ascribe to Moses, Plato, and Milton is that they set at naught books and traditions, and spoke not what others thought, but what they thought. One should learn to detect and watch that gleam of light which flashes across their mind from within, more than the luster of the firmament of bards and sages. Yet they dismiss without notice their thought, because it is their own. In every work of genius we recognize our own rejected thoughts; they come back to us with a certain alienated majesty. Great works of art have no more affecting lesson for us than this. They teach us to abide by our spontaneous impression with good-humored inflexibility then most when the whole cry of voices is on the other side. Else tomorrow a stranger will say with masterly good sense precisely what we have thought and felt all the time, and we shall be forced to take with shame our own opinion from another.

There is a time in everyone's education when they arrive at the conviction that envy is ignorance; that imitation is suicide; that they must take themselves for better or for worse as their portion; that though the wide universe is full of good, no kernel of nourishing corn can come to them but through their toil bestowed on that plot of ground which is given to them to till. The power which resides in them is new in nature, and only they know what that is which they can do, nor do they know until they have tried. Not for nothing one face, one character, one fact, makes much impression on them, and another none. It is not without preestablished harmony, this sculpture in the memory. The eye was placed where one ray should fall, that it might testify of that particular ray. Bravely let him speak the utmost syllable of his confession. We but half express ourselves, and are ashamed of that divine idea which each of us represents. It may be safely trusted as proportionate and of good issues, so it be faithfully imparted, but God will not have such work made manifest by cowards. It needs a divine individual to exhibit anything divine. One can be relieved and gay when they have put their heart into their work and done their best; but what they have said or done otherwise shall give them no peace. It is a deliverance which does not deliver. In the attempt a person's genius deserts them; no muse befriends; no invention, no hope.

Trust thyself: Every heart vibrates to that iron string. Accept the place the divine providence has found for you, the society of your contemporaries, the connection of events. The great have always done so, and confided themselves childlike to the genius of their age, betraying their perception that the Eternal was stirring at their heart, working through their hands, predominating in all their being. And we are now as they, and must accept in the highest mind the same transcendent destiny; and not pinched in a corner, not cowards fleeing before a revolution, but redeemers and benefactors, pious aspirants to be noble clay under the Almighty effort let us advance on Chaos and the Dark.

What pretty oracles nature yields us on this text in the face and behavior of children, babes, and even brutes. That divided and rebel mind, that distrust of a sentiment because our arithmetic has computed the strength and means opposed to our purpose, these have not. Their mind being whole, their eye is as yet unconquered, and when we look in their faces, we are disconcerted. Infancy conforms to nobody; all conform to it; so that one babe commonly makes four or five out of the adults who prattle and play to it. So God has armed youth and puberty and maturity no less with its own piquancy and charm, and made it enviable and gracious and its claims not to be put by, it will stand by itself. Do not think the youth has no force, because they cannot speak to you and me. Hark! in the next room who spoke so clear and emphatic? It seems they know how to speak to their contemporaries. Bashful or bold then, they will know how to make us seniors very unnecessary.

The nonchalance of the young who are sure of a dinner, and would disdain as much as a lord to do or say aught to conciliate one, is the healthy attitude of human nature. How is a child the master of society; independent, irresponsible, looking out from their corner on such people and facts as pass by, they try and sentence them on their merits, in the swift, summary way of children, as good, bad, interesting, silly, eloquent, troublesome. They cumber themselves never about consequences, about interests; they give an independent, genuine verdict. You must court them; they do not court you. But the adult is as it were clapped into jail by their consciousness. As soon as they have once acted or spoken with eclat they are a committed person, watched by the sympathy or the hatred of hundreds, whose affections must now enter into his account. There is no Lethe for this. Ah, that they could pass again into their neutral, godlike independence! Who can thus lose all pledge and, having observed, observe again from the same unaffected, unbiased, unbribable, unaffrighted innocence, must always be formidable, must always engage the poet's and the individual's regards. Of such an immortal youth the force would be felt. They would utter opinions on all passing affairs, which being seen to be not private but necessary, would sink like darts into the ears of others and put them in fear.

These are the voices which we hear in solitude, but they grow faint and inaudible as we enter into the world. Society everywhere is in conspiracy against the fortitude of every one of its members. Society is a joint-stock company, in which the members agree, for the better securing of bread to each shareholder, to surrender the liberty and culture of the eater. The virtue in most requests is conformity. Self-reliance is its aversion. It loves not realities and creators, but names and customs.

Whoso would be self-made, must be a nonconformist. Those who would gather immortal palms must not be hindered by the name of goodness, but must explore if it be goodness. Nothing is at last sacred but the integrity of our own mind. Absolve you to yourself, and you shall have the suffrage of the world. I remember an answer which when quite young I was prompted to make to a valued adviser who was wont to importune me with the dear old doctrines of the church. On my saying, What have I to do with the sacredness of traditions, if I live wholly from within? my friend suggested—"But these impulses may be from below, not from above." I replied, "They do not seem to me to be such; but if I am the devil's child, I will live then from the devil." No law can be sacred to me but that of my nature. Good and bad are but names very readily transferable to that or this; the only right is what is after my constitution; the only wrong what is against it. One must carry themselves in the presence of all opposition as if everything were titular and ephemeral but them. I am ashamed to think how easily we capitulate to badges and names, to large societies and dead institutions. Every decent and well-spoken individual affects and sways me more than is right. I ought to go upright and vital, and speak the rude truth in all ways. If malice and vanity wear the coat of philanthropy, shall that pass? If an angry bigot assumes this bountiful cause of Abolition, and comes to me with his last news from Barbados, why should I not say to him, "Go love thy infant; love thy wood-chopper; be good-natured and modest; have that grace; and never varnish your hard, uncharitable ambition with this incredible tenderness for black folk a thousand miles off. Thy love afar is spite at home." Rough and graceless would be such greeting, but truth is handsomer than the affectation of love. Your goodness must have some edge to it—else it is none. The doctrine of hatred must be preached, as the counteraction of the doctrine of love, when that pules and whines. I shun father and mother and wife and brother when my genius calls me. I would write on the lintels of the doorpost, Whim. I hope it is somewhat better than whim at last, but we cannot spend the day in explanation. Expect me not to show cause why I seek or why I exclude company. Then, again, do not tell me, as someone did today, of my obligation to put all the poor in good situations. Are they my poor? I tell thee, thou foolish philanthropist, that I grudge the dollar, the dime, the cent I give to such others as do not belong to me and to whom I do not belong. There is a class of persons to whom by all spiritual affinity I am bought and sold; for them I will go to prison if need be; but your miscellaneous popular charities; the education at college of fools; the building of meeting-houses to the vain end to which many now stand; alms to sots, and the thousandfold Relief Societies—though I confess with shame I sometimes succumb and give the dollar, it is a wicked dollar, which by-and-by I shall have the strength to withhold.

Virtues are, in the popular estimate, rather the exception than the rule. There are certain people and their virtues. They do what is called a good action, as some piece of courage or charity, much as they would pay a fine in expiation of daily non-appearance on parade. Their works are done as an apology or extenuation of their living in the world—as invalids and the insane pay a high board. Their virtues are penances. I do not wish to expiate, but to live. My life is not an apology, but a life. It is for itself and not for a spectacle. I much prefer that it should be of a lower strain, so it be genuine and equal, than that it should be glittering and unsteady. I wish it to be sound and sweet, and not to need diet and bleeding. My life should be unique; it should be an alms, a battle, a conquest, a medicine. I ask primary evidence that you are a human, and refuse this appeal from another to their actions. I know that for myself it makes no difference whether I do or forbear those actions which are reckoned excellent. I cannot consent to pay for a privilege where I have intrinsic right. Few and mean as my gifts may be, I actually am, and do not need for my own assurance or the assurance of my fellows any secondary testimony.

What I must do is all that concerns me, not what the people think. This rule, equally arduous in actual and in intellectual life, may serve for the whole distinction between greatness and meanness. It is the harder because you will always find those who think they know what is your duty better than you know it. It is easy in the world to live after the world's opinion; it is easy in solitude to live after our own; but the great are those who in the midst of the crowd keep with perfect sweetness the independence of solitude.

The objection to conforming to usages that have become dead to you is that it scatters your force. It loses your time and blurs the impression of your character. If you maintain a dead church, contribute to a dead Bible Society, vote with a great party either for the Government or against it, spread your table like base housekeepers—under all these screens I have difficulty to detect the precise person you are. And of course so much force is withdrawn from your proper life. But do your thing, and I shall know you. Do your work, and you shall reinforce yourself. One must consider what a blindman's buff is this game of conformity. If I know your sect I anticipate your argument. I hear a preacher announce for his text and topic the expediency of one of the institutions of his church. Do I not know beforehand that not possibly can he say a new and spontaneous word? Do I not know that with all this ostentation of examining the grounds of the institution he will do no such thing? Do I not know that he is pledged to himself not to look but at one side, the permitted side, not as a man, but as a parish minister? He is a retained attorney, and these airs of the bench are the emptiest affectation. Well, most have bound their eyes with one or another handkerchief, and attached themselves to some one of these communities of opinion. This conformity makes them not false in a few particulars, authors of a few lies, but false in all particulars. Their every truth is not quite true. Their two is not the real two, their four not the real four: So that every word they say chagrins us and we know not where to begin to set them right. Meantime nature is not slow to equip us in the prison-uniform of the party to which we adhere. We come to wear one cut of face and figure, and acquire by degrees the gentlest asinine expression. There is a mortifying experience in particular, which does not fail to wreak itself also in the general history; I mean "the foolish face of praise," the forced smile which we put on in company where we do not feel at ease, in answer to conversation which does not interest us. The muscles, not spontaneously moved but moved by a low usurping willfulness, grow tight about the outline of the face, and make the most disagreeable sensation; a sensation of rebuke and warning which no brave young man will suffer twice.

For nonconformity the world whips you with its displeasure. And therefore one must know how to estimate a sour face. The bystanders look askance on that person in the public street or in the friend's parlor. If this aversion had its origin in contempt and resistance like one's own, they might well go home with a sad countenance; but the sour faces of the multitude, like their sweet faces, have no deep cause—disguise no god, but are put on and off as the wind blows and a newspaper directs. Yet is the discontent of the multitude more formidable than that of the senate and the college. It is easy enough for the stronghearted who know the world to brook the rage of the cultivated classes. Their rage is decorous and prudent, for they are timid, as being very vulnerable themselves. But when to their rage the indignation of the people is added, when the ignorant and the poor are aroused, when the unintelligent brute force that lies at the bottom of society is made to growl and mow, it needs the habit of magnanimity and religion to treat it godlike as a trifle of no concernment.

The other terror that scares us from self-trust is our consistency; a reverence for our past act or word because the eyes of others have no other data for computing our orbit than our past acts, and we are loathe to disappoint them.

But why should you keep your head over your shoulder? Why drag about this monstrous corpse of your memory, lest you contradict somewhat you have stated in this or that public place? Suppose you should contradict yourself; what then? It seems to be a rule of wisdom never to rely on your memory alone, scarcely even in acts of pure memory, but to bring the past for judgment into the thousand-eyed present, and live ever in a new day. Trust your emotion. In your metaphysics you have denied personality to the Deity, yet when the devout motions of the soul come, yield to them heart and life, though they should clothe God with shape and color. Leave your theory, as Joseph his coat in the hand of the harlot, and flee.

A foolish consistency is the hobgoblin of little minds, adored by little statesmen and philosophers and divines. With consistency a great soul has simply nothing to do. They may as well concern themselves with his shadow on the wall. Out upon your guarded lips! Sew them up with packthread, do. Else if you would be one to speak what you think today in words as hard as cannon balls, and tomorrow speak what tomorrow thinks in hard words again, though it contradict everything you said today. Ah, then, exclaim the aged, you shall be sure to be misunderstood! Misunderstood! It is a right fool's word. Is it so bad then to be misunderstood? Pythagoras was misunderstood, and Socrates, and Jesus, and Luther, and Copernicus, and Galileo, and Newton, and every pure and wise spirit that ever took flesh. To be great is to be misunderstood.

I suppose no one can violate his nature. All the sallies of their will are rounded in by the law of their being, as the inequalities of Andes and Himmaleh are insignificant in the curve of the sphere. Nor does it matter how you gauge and try them. A character is like an acrostic or Alexandrian stanza—read it forward, backward, or across, it still spells the same thing. In this pleasing contrite wood-life which God allows me, let me record day by day my honest thought without prospect or retrospect, and I cannot doubt, it will be found symmetrical, though I mean it not and see it not. My book should smell of pines and resound with the hum of insects. The swallow over my window should interweave that thread or straw it carries in its bill into my web also. We pass for what we are. Character teaches above our wills. Many people imagine that they communicate their virtue or vice only by overt actions, and do not see that virtue or vice emit a breath every moment.

Fear never but you shall be consistent in whatever variety of actions, so they be each honest and natural in their hour. For of one will, the actions will be harmonious, however unlike they seem. These varieties are lost sight of when seen at a little distance, at a little height of thought. One tendency unites them all. The voyage of the best ship is a zigzag line of a hundred tacks. This is only microscopic criticism. See the line from a sufficient distance, and it straightens itself to the average tendency. Your genuine action will explain itself and will explain your other genuine actions. Your conformity explains nothing. Act singly, and what you have already done singly will justify you now. Greatness always appeals to the future. If I can be great enough now to do right and scorn eyes, I must have done so much right before as to defend me now. Be it how it will, do right now. Always scorn appearances and you always may. The force of character is cumulative. All the foregone days of virtue work their health into this. What makes the majesty of the heroes of the senate and the field, which so fills the imagination? The consciousness of a train of great days and victories behind. There they all stand and shed a united light on the advancing actor. They are attended as by a visible escort of angels to everyone's eye. That is it which throws thunder into Chatham's voice, and dignity into Washington's port, and America into Adams' eye. Honor is venerable to us because it is no ephemeris. It is always ancient virtue. We worship it today because it is not of today. We love it and pay it homage because it is not a trap for our love and homage, but is self-dependent, self-derived, and therefore of an old immaculate pedigree, even if shown in a young person.

I hope in these days we have heard the last of conformity and consistency. Let the words be gazetted and ridiculous henceforward. Instead of the gong for dinner, let us hear a whistle from the Spartan fife. Let us bow and apologize never more. A great man is coming to eat at my house. I do not wish to please him: I wish that he should wish to please me. I will stand here for humanity, and though I would make it kind, I would make it true.

Let us affront and reprimand the smooth mediocrity and squalid contentment of the times, and hurl in the face of custom and trade and office, the fact which is the upshot of all history, that there is a great responsible Thinker and Actor moving wherever one moves; that a true individual belongs to no other time or place, but is the center of things. Where the soul resides, there is nature. The Thinker and Actor measures you and all others and all events. You are constrained to accept that standard. Ordinarily, everybody in society reminds us of somewhat else, or of some other person. Character, reality, reminds you of nothing else; it takes place of the whole creation. One must be so that they must make all circumstances indifferent—put all means into the shade. This all great people are and do. Every true individual is a cause, a country, and an age; requires infinite spaces and numbers and time fully to accomplish their thought—and posterity seems to follow their steps as a procession. A man Cæsar is born, and for ages after we have a Roman Empire. Christ is born, and millions of minds so grow and cleave to His genius that He is confounded with virtue and the possible of all. An institution is the lengthened shadow of the founder; as, the Reformation, of Luther; Quakerism, of Fox; Methodism, of Wesley; Abolition, of Clarkson. Scipio, Milton called "the height of Rome"; and all history resolves itself very easily into the biography of a few stout and earnest persons.

Let all people then know their worth, and keep things under their feet. Let them not peep or steal, or skulk up and down with the air of a charity-boy, a bastard, or an interloper in the world which exists for them. But the commoner in the street, finding no worth in themselves which corresponds to the force which built a tower or sculptured a marble god, feels poor when looking upon these. To them a palace, a statue, or a costly book have an alien and forbidding air, much like a gay equipage, and seem to say like that, "Who are you?" Yet they all are theirs, suitors for their notice, petitioners to their faculties that they will come out and take possession. The picture waits for my verdict; it is not to command me, but I am to settle its claim to praise. That popular fable of the sot—who was picked up dead drunk in the street, carried to the duke's house, washed and dressed and laid in the duke's bed, and, on his waking, treated with all obsequious ceremony like the duke, and assured that he had been insane—owes its popularity to the fact that it symbolizes so well the state of one and all, who are in the world a sort of sot, but now and then wakes up, exercises their reason, and finds themselves truly blessed.

Our reading is mendicant and sycophantic. In history our imagination makes fools of us, plays us false.

Kingdom and lordship, power and estate, are a gaudier vocabulary than private John and Edward in a small house and common day's work—but the things of life are the same to both: the sum total of both is the same. Why all this deference to Alfred and Scanderbeg and Gustavus? Suppose they were virtuous; did they wear out virtue? As great a stake depends on your private act today as followed their public and renowned steps. When private individuals shall act with original views, the luster will be transferred from the actions of monarchs to those of ordinary people.

The world has indeed been instructed by its leaders, who have so magnetized the eyes of nations. It has been taught by this colossal symbol the mutual reverence that is due from one and all. The joyful loyalty with which people have everywhere suffered under a monarchy, the noble, or the great proprietor to walk among them by a law of its own, make its own scale of subjects and things and reverse theirs, pay for benefits not with money but with honor, and represent the Law of a king, was the hieroglyphic by which the subjects obscurely signified their consciousness of their own right and comeliness, the right of every ordinary person.

The magnetism which all original action exerts is explained when we inquire the reason of self-trust.

Who is the Trustee? What is the aboriginal Self, on which a universal reliance may be grounded? What is the nature and power of that science-baffling star, without parallax, without calculable elements, which shoots a ray of beauty even into trivial and impure actions, if the least mark of independence appear? The inquiry leads us to that source, at once the essence of genius, the essence of virtue, and the essence of life, which we call Spontaneity or Instinct. We denote this primary wisdom as Intuition, whilst all later teachings are tuitions. In that deep force, the last fact behind which analysis cannot go, all things find their common origin. For the sense of being which in calm hours rises, we know not how, in the soul, is not diverse from things, from space from light, from time, from others, but one with them and proceedeth obviously from the same source whence their life and being also proceedeth. We first share the life by which things exist and afterwards see them as appearances in nature and forget that we have shared their cause. Here is the fountain of action and the fountain of thought. Here are the lungs of that inspiration which giveth people wisdom, of that inspiration which cannot be denied without impiety and atheism. We lie in the lap of immense intelligence, which makes us organs of its activity and receivers of its truth. When we discern justice, when we discern truth, we do nothing of ourselves, but allow a passage to its beams. If we ask whence this comes, if we seek to pry into the soul that causes—all metaphysics, all philosophy is at fault. Its presence or its absence is all we can affirm. All people discern between the voluntary acts of their mind and their involuntary perceptions. And to their involuntary perceptions they know a perfect respect is due. One may err in the expression of them, but they know that these things are so, like day and night, not to be disputed. All my willful actions and acquisitions are but roving—the most trivial reverie, the faintest native emotion, are domestic and divine. Thoughtless people contradict as readily the statement of perceptions as of opinions, or rather much more readily; for they do not distinguish between perception and notion. They fancy that I choose to see this or that thing. But perception is not whimsical, but fatal. If I see a trait, my children will see it after me, and in course of time all people— although it may chance that no one has seen it before me. For my perception of it is as much a fact as the sun.

The relations of the soul to the divine spirit are so pure that it is profane to seek to interpose helps . It must be that when God speaketh it, communication should not be on one thing, but all things; should fill the world with only God's voice; should scatter forth light, nature, time, souls, from the center of the present thought;

thus creating a new whole. Whenever a mind is simple and receives a divine wisdom, then old things pass away—means, teachers, texts, temples fall; it lives now, and absorbs past and future into the present hour. All things are made sacred by relation to it—one thing as much as another. All things are dissolved to their center by their cause, and in the universal miracle petty and particular miracles disappear. This is and must be. If therefore anyone claims to know and speak of God and carries you backward to the phraseology of some old mouldered nation in another country, in another world, believe them not. Is the acorn better than the oak which is its fullness and completion? Is the parent better than the child into whom they have cast their ripened being? Whence then this worship of the past? The centuries are conspirators against the sanity and majesty of the soul. Time and space are but physiological colors which the eye maketh, but the soul is light; where it is, is day; where it was, is night; and history is an impertinence and an injury if it be anything more than a cheerful apologue or parable of my being and becoming.

Humans are by nature timid and apologetic; we are no longer upright; we dare not say "I think," "I am," but quote some saint or sage. We are ashamed before the blade of grass or the blowing rose. These roses under my window make no reference to former roses or to better ones; they are for what they are; they exist with God today. There is no time to them. There is simply the rose; it is perfect in every moment of its existence. Before a leaf-bud has burst, its whole life acts; in the full-blown flower there is no more; in the leafless root there is no less. Its nature is satisfied and it satisfies nature in all moments alike. There is no time to it. But people postpone or remember; they do not live in the present, but with reverted eye lament the past, or, heedless of the riches that surround them, stand on tiptoe to fore-see the future. They cannot be happy and strong until they too live with nature in the present, above time.

This should be plain enough. Yet see what strong intellects dare not yet hear the voice of God unless those words speak the phraseology of I know not what David, or Jeremiah, or Paul. We shall not always set so great a price on a few texts, on a few lives. We are like children who repeat by rote the sentences of gran-dames and tutors, and, as they grow older, of the influ-ence of others whose talents and character they chance to see—painfully recollecting the exact words they spoke; afterwards, when they come into the point of view which those had who uttered these sayings, they understand them and are willing to let the words go; for at any time they can use words as good when occasion comes. So was it with us, so will it be, if we proceed. If we live truly, we shall see truly. It is as easy for the strong to be strong, as it is for the weak to be weak. When we have new perception, we shall gladly disburthen the memory of its hoarded treasures as old rubbish. When one lives with God, that voice shall be as sweet as the murmur of the brook and the rustle of the corn.

And now at last the highest truth on this subject remains unsaid; probably cannot be said; for all that we say is the far off remembering of the intuition. That thought, by what I can now nearest approach to say it, is this. When good is near you, when you have life in yourself—it is not by any known or appointed way; you shall not discern the footprints of any other; you shall not see the face of humanity; you shall not hear any name—the way, the thought, the good, shall be wholly strange and new. It shall exclude all other being. You take the way *from* mankind, not to mankind. All persons that ever existed are its fugitive ministers. There shall be no fear in it. Fear and hope are alike beneath it. It asks nothing. There is somewhat low even in hope. We are then in vision. There is nothing that can be called gratitude, nor properly joy. The soul is raised over passion. It seeth identity and eternal causation. It is a perceiving that Truth and Right are. Hence it becomes a Tranquillity out of the knowing that all things go well. Vast spaces of nature; the Atlantic Ocean, the South

Sea; vast intervals of time, years, centuries, are of no account. This which I think and feel underlay that former state of life and circumstances, as it does underlie my present and will always all circumstances, and what is called life and what is called death.

Life only avails, not the having lived. Power ceases in the instant of repose; it resides in the moment of transition from a past to a new state, in the shooting of the gulf, in the darting to an aim. This one fact the world hates, that the soul *becomes*; for that forever degrades the past; turns all riches to poverty, all reputation to a shame; confounds the saint with the rogue; shoves Jesus and Judas equally aside. Why then do we prate of self-reliance? Inasmuch as the soul is present there will be power not confident but agent. To talk of reliance is a poor external way of speaking. Speak rather of that which relies because it works and is. Who has more soul than I masters me, though should not be done with a raised finger. From within I must revolve by the gravitation of spirits. Who has less I rule with like facility. We fancy it rhetoric when we speak of eminent virtue. We do not yet see that virtue is Height, and that an individual or a company of others, plastic and permeable to principles, by the law of nature must overpower and ride all cities, nations, leaders, the rich, poets, who are not.

This is the ultimate fact which we so quickly reach

on this, as on every topic, the resolution of all into the ever-blessed ONE. Virtue is the governor, the creator, the reality. All things real are so by so much virtue as they contain. Hardship, farming, hunting, whaling, war, eloquence, personal weight, are somewhat, and engage my respect as examples of the soul's presence and impure action. I see the same law working in nature for conservation and growth. The poise of a planet, the bended tree recovering itself from the strong wind, the vital resources of every animal and vegetable, are also demonstrations of the self-sufficing and therefore self-relying soul. All history, from its highest to its trivial passages, is the various record of this power.

Thus all concentrates; let us not rove; let us sit at home with the cause. Let us stun and astonish the intruding rabble of the outspoken and books and institutions by a simple declaration of the divine fact. Bid them take the shoes from off their feet, for God is here within. Let our simplicity judge them, and our docility to our own law demonstrate the poverty of nature and fortune beside our native riches.

But now we are a mob. We do not stand in awe of ourselves, nor do we admonish genius to stay at home, to put itself in communication with the internal ocean, but go abroad to beg a cup of water of the urns of others. We must go alone. Isolation must precede true society. I like the silent church before the service begins, better than any preaching. How far off, how cool, how chaste the people look, begirt each one with a precinct or sanctuary. So let us always sit. Why should we assume the faults of our friend, or wife, or father, or child, because they sit around our hearth, or are said to have the same blood? All have my blood and I have all others'. Not for that will I adopt their petulance or folly, even to the extent of being ashamed of it. But your isolation must not be mechanical, but spiritual, that is, must be elevation.

At times the whole world seems to be in conspiracy to importune you with emphatic trifles. Friend, client, child, sickness, fear, want, charity, all knock at once at thy closet door and say, "Come out unto us." Do not spill thy soul; do not all descend; keep thy state; stay at home in thine own heaven; come not for a moment into their facts, into their hubbub of conflicting appearances, but let in the light of thy law on their confusion. The power others possess to annoy me I give them by a weak curiosity. No one can come near me but through my act. "What we love that we have, but by desire we bereave ourselves of the love."

If we cannot at once rise to the sanctities of obedience and faith, let us at least resist our temptations, let us enter into the state of war and wake Thor and Woden, courage and constancy, in our Saxon breasts. This is to be done in our smooth times by speaking the truth. Check this lying hospitality and lying affection. Live no longer to the expectation of these deceived and deceiving people with whom we converse. Say to them, O father, O mother, O sister, O brother, O friend, I have lived with you after appearances hitherto. Henceforward I am the truth's. Be it known unto you that henceforward I obey no law less than the eternal law. I will have no covenants but proximities. I shall endeavor to nourish my parents, to support my family, to be the chaste husband of one wife—but these relations I must fill after a new and unprecedented way. I appeal from your customs. I must be myself. I cannot break myself any longer for you, or you. If you can love me for what I am, we shall be happier. If you cannot, I will still seek to deserve that you should. I must be myself. I will not hide my tastes or aversions. I will so trust that what is deep is holy, that I will do strongly before the sun and moon whatever inly rejoices me and the heart appoints. If you are noble, I will love you; if you are not, I will not hurt you and myself by hypocritical attentions. If you are true, but not in the same truth with me, cleave to your companions; I will seek my own. I do this not selfishly but humbly and truly. It is alike your interest, and mine, and all others, however long we have dwelt in lies, to live in truth. Does this sound harsh today? You will soon love what is dictated by your nature as well as mine, and if we follow the truth it will bring us out safe at last. But so may you give these friends pain. Yes, but I cannot sell my liberty and my power, to save their sensibility. Besides, all persons have their moments of reason, when they look out into the region of absolute truth; then will they justify me and do the same thing.

The populace think that your rejection of popular standards is a rejection of all standard, and mere anti-nomianism; and the bold sensualist will use the name of philosophy to gild his crimes. But the law of conscious-ness abides. There are two confessionals, in one or the other of which we must be shriven. You may fulfill your round of duties by clearing yourself in the *direct*, or in the *reflex* way. Consider whether you have satisfied your relations to father, mother, cousin, neighbor, town, cat and dog; whether any of these can upbraid you. But I may also neglect this reflex standard and absolve me to myself. I have my own stern claims and perfect circle. It denies the name of duty to many offices that are called duties. But if I can discharge its debts it enables me to dispense with the popular code. If any one imagines that this law is lax, let them keep its commandment one day.

And truly it demands something godlike in those who have cast off the common motives of humanity and have ventured to trust themselves for a taskmaster. High be their heart, faithful their will, clear their sight, that they may in good earnest be doctrine, society, law, to themselves, that a simple purpose may be to them as strong as iron necessity is to others.

If one considers the present aspects of what is called by distinction *society*, they will see the need of these ethics. The sinew and heart of all people seem to be drawn out, and we become timorous desponding whimperers. We are afraid of truth, afraid of fortune, afraid of death, and afraid of each other. Our age yields no great and perfect persons. We want men and women who shall renovate life and our social state, but we see that most natures are insolvent; cannot satisfy their own wants, have an ambition out of all proportion to their practical force, and so do lean and beg day and night continually. Our housekeeping is mendicant, our arts, our occupations, our marriages, our religion we have not chosen, but society has chosen for us. We are parlor soldiers. The rugged battle of fate, where strength is born, we shun.

If our young miscarry in their first enterprises they lose all heart. If the young merchant fails, some say they are ruined. If the finest genius studies at one of our colleges, and is not installed in an office within one year afterwards, in the cities or suburbs of Boston or

New York, it seems to his friends and to himself that he is right in being disheartened and in complaining the rest of his life. A sturdy lad from New Hamsphire or Vermont, who in turn tries all the professions, who teams it, farms it, peddles, keeps a school, preaches, edits a newspaper, goes to Congress, buys a township, and so forth, in successive years, and always like a cat falls on his feet, is worth a hundred of these city dolls. He walks abreast with his days and feels no shame in not "studying a profession," for he does not postpone his life, but lives already. He has not one chance, but a hundred chances. Let a stoic arise who shall reveal the resources of all and tell them they are not leaning willows, but can and must detach themselves; that with the exercise of self-trust, new powers shall appear; that in everyone is the word made flesh, born to shed healing to the nations, that they should be ashamed of our compassion, and that the moment they act of their own will, tossing the laws, the books, idolatries and customs out of the window—we pity them no more but thank and revere them—and that teacher shall restore their life to splendor and make their name dear to all History.

It is easy to see that a greater self-reliance—a new respect for the divinity in all—must work a revolution in all the offices and relations of all people; in their religion; in their education; in their pursuits; their modes of living; their association; in their property; in their speculative views.

1. In what prayers do individuals allow themselves! That which they call a holy office is not so much as brave and gallant. Prayer looks abroad and asks for some foreign addition to come through some foreign virtue, and loses itself in endless mazes of natural and supernatural, and mediatorial and miraculous. Prayer that craves a particular commodity, anything less than all good, is vicious. Prayer is the contemplation of the facts of life from the highest point of view. It is the soliloquy of a beholding and jubilant soul. It is the spirit pronouncing the greatness of God's good works. But prayer as a means to effect a private end is meanness and theft. It supposes dualism and not unity in nature and consciousness. As soon as we are at one with God, we will not beg. We will then see prayer in all action. The prayer of the farmer kneeling in his field to weed it, the prayer of the rower kneeling with the stroke of his oar, are true prayers heard throughout nature, though for cheap ends. Caratach, in Fletcher's Bonduca, when admonished to inquire the mind of the god Audate, replies—

"His hidden meaning lies in our endeavors;
Our valors are our best gods."

Another sort of false prayers are our regrets.

Discontent is the want of self-reliance: It is infirmity of will. Regret calamities if you can thereby help the sufferer; if not, attend your own work and already the evil begins to be repaired. Our sympathy is just as base. We come to them who weep foolishly and sit down and cry for company, instead of imparting to them truth and health in rough electric shocks, putting them once more in communication with their own reason. The secret of fortune is joy in our hands. Welcome evermore to gods and humanity is the self-helping sort. For them all doors are flung wide; them all tongues greet, all honors crown, all eyes follow with desire. Our love goes out to them and embraces them because they did not need it. We solicitously and apologetically caress and celebrate them because they held on their way and scorned our disapprobation. The gods love them because others hated them. "To the persevering mortal," said Zoroaster, "the blessed Immortals are swift."

As one's prayers are a disease of the will, so are their creeds a disease of the intellect. They say with those foolish Israelites, "Let not God speak to us, lest we die. Speak thou, speak any man with us, and we will obey." Everywhere I am hindered of meeting God in those around me, because they have shut their own temple doors and recite fables merely of their elders, or their elder's elders God. Every new mind is a new classification. If it prove a mind of uncommon activity and power, a Locke, a Lavoisier, a Hutton, a Bentham, a Fourier, it imposes its classification on others, and lo! a new system. In proportion to the depth of the thought, and so to the number of the objects it touches and brings within reach of the pupil, is their complacency. But chiefly is this apparent in creeds and churches, which are also classifications of some powerful mind acting on the elemental thought of duty, and its relation to the Highest. Such is Calvinism, Quakerism, Swedenborgism. The pupil takes the same delight in subordinating everything to the new terminology as someone who has just learned botany in seeing a new earth and new seasons thereby. It will happen for a time that the pupil will find their intellectual power has grown by the study of their master's mind. But in all unbalanced minds the classification is idolized, passes for the end and not for a speedily exhaustible means, so that the walls of the system blend to their eye in the remote horizon with the walls of the universe; the luminaries of heaven seem to them hung on the arch their master built. They cannot imagine how you aliens have any right to see—how you can see; "It must be somehow that you stole the light from us." They do not yet perceive that light, unsystematic, indomitable, will break into any cabin, even into theirs. Let them chirp awhile and call it their own. If they are honest and do well, presently their neat new pinfold will be too straight and low, will crack, will lean, will rot and vanish, and the immortal light, all young and joyful, million-orbed, million-colored, will beam over the universe as on the first morning.

2. It is for want of self-culture that the superstition of Travelling, whose idols are Italy, England, Egypt, retains its fascination for all educated Americans. They who made England, Italy, or Greece venerable in the imagination did so by sticking fast where they were, like an axis of the earth. In manly hours we feel that duty is our place. The soul is no traveller; the wise man stays at home, and when his necessities, his duties, on any occasion call him from his house, or into foreign lands, he is at home still, and shall make men sensible by the expression of his countenance that he goes, the missionary of wisdom and virtue, and visit cities like a sovereign and not like an interloper or a valet. I have no churlish objection to the circumnavigation of the globe for the purposes of art, of study, and benevolence, so that the individual is first domesticated, or does not go abroad with the hope of finding somewhat greater than they know. Those who travel to be amused, or to get somewhat which they do not carry, travel away from themselves, and grow old even in youth among old things. In Thebes, in Palmyra, their will and mind have become old and dilapidated as they. Thus they carry ruins to ruins.

Travelling is a fool's paradise. Our first journeys discover to us the indifference of places. At home I dream that at Naples, at Rome, I can be intoxicated with beauty and lose my sadness. I pack my trunk, embrace my friends, embark on the sea and at last wake up in Naples, and there beside me is the stern fact, the sad self, unrelenting, identical, that I fled from. I seek the Vatican and the palaces. I affect to be intoxicated with sights and suggestions, but I am not intoxicated. My giant goes with me wherever I go.

3. But the rage of travelling is a symptom of a deeper unsoundness affecting the whole intellectual action. The intellect is vagabond, and our system of education fosters restlessness. Our minds travel when our bodies are forced to stay at home. We imitate; and what is imitation but the travelling of the mind? Our houses are built with foreign taste; our shelves are garnished with foreign ornaments; our opinions, our tastes, our faculties, lean, and follow the Past and the Distant. The soul created the arts wherever they have flourished. It was in the artist's own mind that the artist sought a model. It was an application of their own thought to the thing to be done and the conditions to be observed. And why need we copy the Doric or the Gothic model? Beauty, convenience, grandeur of thought and quaint expression are as near to us as to any, and if the American artist will study with hope and love the precise thing to be done, considering the climate, the soil, the length of the day, the wants of the people, the habit and form of the government, the American will create a house in which all these will find themselves fitted, and taste and sentiment will be satisfied also.

Insist on yourself; never imitate. Your own gift you can present every moment with the cumulative force of a whole life's cultivation; but of the adopted talent of another you have only an extemporaneous half possession. That which each can do best, none but their Maker can teach them. No one yet knows what it is, nor can, till that person has exhibited it. Where is the master who could have taught Shakespeare? Where is the master who could have instructed Franklin, or Washington, or Bacon, or Newton? Every great pioneer is unique. The Scipionism of Scipio is precisely that part he could not borrow. Shakespeare will never be made by the study of Shakespeare. Do that which is assigned you, and you cannot hope too much or dare too much. There is at this moment for you an utterance brave and grand as that of the colossal chisel of Phidias, or trowel of the Egyptians, or the pen of Moses or Dante, but different from all these. Not possibly will the soul, all rich, all eloquent, with thousand-cloven tongue, deign to repeat itself; but if you can hear what these patriarchs say, surely you can reply to them in the same pitch of voice; for the ear and the tongue are two organs of one nature. Abide in the simple and noble regions of thy life, obey thy heart and thou shalt reproduce the Foreworld again.

4. As our Religion, our Education, our Art look abroad, so does our spirit of society. All people plume themselves on the improvement of society, and no individual improves.

Society never advances. It recedes as fast on one side as it gains on the other. Its progress is only apparent like the workers of a treadmill. It undergoes continual changes; it is barbarous, it is civilized, it is christianized, it is rich, it is scientific; but this change is not amelioration. For everything that is given something is taken. Society acquires new arts and loses old instincts. What a contrast between the well-clad, reading, writing, thinking American, with a watch, a pencil, and a bill of exchange in his pocket, and the naked New Zealander, whose property is a club, a spear, a mat, and an undivided twentieth of a shed to sleep under. But compare the health of the two men and you see that his aboriginal strength, the white man has lost. If the traveller tell us truly, strike the savage with a broad axe and in a day or two the flesh shall unite and heal as if you struck the blow into soft pitch, and the same blow shall send the white man to his grave.

The civilized man has built a coach, but has lost the use of his feet. He is supported on crutches, but lacks so much support of muscle. He has got a fine Geneva watch, but he has lost the skill to tell the hour by the sun. A Greenwich nautical almanac he has, and so being sure of the information when he wants it, the man in the street does not know a star in the sky. The solstice he does not observe; the equinox he knows as little; and the whole bright calendar of the year is without a dial in his mind. His notebooks impair his memory; his libraries overload his wit; the insurance-office increases the number of accidents; and it may be a question whether machinery does not encumber; whether we have not lost by refinement some energy, by a Christianity entrenched in establishments and forms some vigor of wild virtue. For every stoic was a stoic; but in Christendom where is the Christian?

There is no more deviation in the moral standard than in the standard of height or bulk. No greater individuals are now than ever were. A singular equality may be observed between the great societies of the first and of the last ages; nor can all the science, art, religion, and philosophy of the nineteenth century avail to educate greater beings than Plutarch's heroes, three or four and twenty centuries ago. Not in time is the race progressive. Phocion, Socrates, Anaxagoras, Diogenes are great, but they leave no class. Those who are really of their class will not be called by their names, but be wholly their own guide, and in their turn the founder of a sect. The arts and inventions of each period are only its costume and do not invigorate all people. The harm of the improved machinery may compensate its good. Hudson and Behring accomplished so much in their fishing-boats as to astonish Parry and Franklin, whose equipment exhausted the resources of science and art. Galileo, with an opera-glass, discovered a more splendid series of facts than any one since. Columbus found the New World in an undecked boat. It is curious to see the periodical disuse and perishing of means and machinery which were introduced with loud laudation a few years or centuries before. The great genius returns to the essential human experience. We reckoned the improvements of the art of war among the triumphs of science, and yet Napoleon conquered Europe by the Bivouac, which consisted of falling back on naked valor and disencumbering it of all aids. The Emperor held it impossible to make a perfect army, says Las Cases, "without abolishing our arms, magazines, commissaries and carriages, until, in imitation of the Roman custom, the soldier should receive his supply of corn, grind it in his hand-mill and bake his bread himself."

Society is a wave. The wave moves onward, but the water of which it is composed does not. The same particle does not rise from the valley to the ridge. Its unity is only phenomenal. The persons who make up a nation today die, and their experience with them.

And so the reliance on Property, including the reliance on governments which protect it, is the want of self-reliance. People have looked away from themselves and at things so long that they have come to esteem what they call the soul's progress, namely, the religious, learned, and civil institutions as guards of property, and they deprecate assaults on these, because they feel them to be assaults on property. They measure their esteem of each other by what each has, and not by what each is. But a cultivated individual becomes ashamed of their property, ashamed of what they have, out of new respect for their being. Especially hating what they have if they see that it is accidental—came to them by inheritance, or gift, or crime; then they feel that it is not having; it does not belong to them, has no root in them,

and merely lies there because no revolution or no robber takes it away. But that which a person is, does always
by necessity acquire, and what that person acquires, is
permanent and living property, which does not wait the
beck of rulers, or mobs, or revolutions, or fire, or storm,
or bankruptcies, but perpetually renews itself wherever
they are put. "Thy lot or portion of life," said the Caliph
Ali, "is seeking after thee; therefore be at rest from seeking after it." Our dependence on these foreign goods
leads us to our slavish respect for numbers. The political parties meet in numerous conventions; the greater
the concourse and with each new uproar of announcement. The delegation from Essex! The Democrats from
New Hampshire! The Whigs of Maine! The young
patriot feels stronger than before by a new abundance
of eyes and arms. In like manner the reformers sum-
mon conventions and vote and resolve in multitude.
But not so O friends! will the God deign to enter and
inhabit you, but by a method precisely the reverse. It is
only as those who put off from themselves all external
support and stand alone that I see them to be strong
and to prevail. They are weaker by every recruit to their
banner. Is not one person better than a town? Ask nothing of others, and, in the endless mutation, thou only
firm column must presently appear the upholder of all
that surrounds thee. The ones who know that power is

in the soul, that they are weak only because they have looked for good outside of themselves and elsewhere, and, so perceiving, throw themselves unhesitatingly on their thought, instantly rights themselves, stands in the erect position, commands their limbs, works miracles; just as one who stands on one's feet is stronger than those who stand on their head.

So use all that is called Fortune. Most others will gamble with it, and gain all, or lose all, as the wheel rolls. But do thou leave as unlawful these winnings, and deal with Cause and Effect, the chancellors of God. In the Will work and acquire, and thou hast chained the wheel of Chance, and shalt always drag it after thee. A political victory, a rise of rents, the recovery of your sick or the return of your absent friend, or some other quite external event raises your spirits, and you think good days are preparing for you. Do not believe it. It can never be so. Nothing can bring you peace but yourself. Nothing can bring you peace but the triumph of principles.

"Whenever a mind is simple
and receives a divine wisdom,
then old things pass away;
means, teachers, texts, temples fall;
it lives now and absorbs past and future
into the present hour."

—Ralph Waldo Emerson

QUESTIONS TO CONSIDER:

1. What does self-reliance mean to you?

2. How does it differ from aloofness and "not needing anyone."

3. What are some ways parents can help their children to be more self-reliant?

4. Imitation is futile. Have you ever tried to be like someone else, only to have it fail?

5. Do you believe we all have a genius potential?

6. What about natural talents? Why do some have musical ability and others can draw well? Does Emerson address this?

7. What happens to you emotionally when you ignore a good idea and then see someone else make it a huge success?

8. How would you describe a nonconformist in today's world? Is it rebellion or simply trusting the self?

9. Ernest Holmes said, "turn away from the facts, seek the Truth." Did you hear that in this essay?

10. What does self-reliance have to do with "rugged individualism"?

The Over-Soul
Emerson the Mystic

Overview:

THE OVER-SOUL OUTLINES EMERSON'S BELIEF
IN A GOD WHO LIVES IN EVERYONE. WE
CAN COMMUNICATE WITH GOD DIRECTLY,
WITHOUT A CHURCH. EMERSON SAYS THAT
EACH PERSON IS A PART OF THE WHOLE
PICTURE BUT REMAINS AN INDIVIDUAL.

"THE OVER-SOUL" IS A FAVORITE ESSAY of many a New Thought student. Emerson opens with a provocative statement: "Our faith comes in moments, our vice is habitual." Those moments of Faith are insights, realizations, the awareness of our Unity in Spirit, our connection to all life. Some call such moments "mystical experience," but they are actually healthy-mindedness. He asserted, "There is a depth in those moments of faith which constrains us to ascribe more reality to them than to all other experiences." There is something in us that knows our true worth is beyond experience. Holmes would speak of our desires as indications of a spiritual prototype, that their fulfillment exists in the "quantum realm of potential."

In other words, we want love and joy and peace and supply because our soul knows they are there for the taking! Christianity would say: "It is the Father's good wish to give you the kingdom." Emerson and Holmes attest: The kingdom is within. Therefore, to reiterate from Self-Reliance: "Be still and know that I am God." Holmes might tweak that a bit, as I have, and state: "Be still and know that I am is God." It follows that God is the greater Self personified as us.

There is an invisible Source for everything. In sentient life, animals and humans, the Source must, by necessity, be conscious as well. Einstein's formula $E=MC^2$, means to us that energy and matter are the same thing; that the invisible and the visible are identical; that the source of the form and the form are One. "Things which appear come from things which do not appear." Since we have an innate intelligence, it follows that the Source is Intelligence. We long for the very things that are part of our nature, love and peace, joy and creative self-expression.

When Emerson says, "Man is a stream whose source is hidden," we must remember the Source is hidden behind the personality, the ego, the local sense of self. We know who we are by what we desire.

There is a Greater Self, which in turn is the expression of a greater Presence, the Over-Soul. "Always our Being is descending into us from we know not where." That reminds me of Meister Eckart, who said: "God is forever begetting the only begotten." This is a key aspect of Holmes' teaching as well; that we are not "created, then left to suffer." No, we are an ongoing individualization of Spirit, whole in our potential but forever drawing from it. We are meant to discover who we are through our own individual expression. The awareness that we are drawing from that ultimate Source, that hidden power, awakens us to our potential.

One of my favorite passages in this essay is when Emerson speaks about the descent of Spirit into matter. "When it breathes through their intellect, it is genius; when it breathes through their will, it is virtue; when it flows through their affections, it is love." That is the best description of How it works and What it does that I have ever heard. Like Emerson, Holmes was aware that "our faith comes in moments." He was very down to earth and admitting of human errors, but he was more attuned to the possibility of our becoming a greater expression of the hidden Source.

Emerson's advice would be to let this subtle presence

have its way through us. This is in accord with the great spiritual traditions of the East, and to some extent of the teachings of Jesus. We are shown the value of inner silence, of slowing the thinking mind, of turning away from the conditions of life. Emerson uses an old quote: "God comes to see us without Bell." It means it is a subtle experience to realize the Presence, more like a dawning than a lightning flash. It is an arising of awareness, a gentle realization.

An interesting part of this essay is when Emerson speaks of the "ascension of the soul to higher states" not being a slow march forward. It is more like a metamorphosis, such as caterpillar into butterfly; rather effortless and natural. The late futurist Barbara Marx Hubbard often said evolution is not a slow process. It happens by leaps.

Emerson speaks of "the heart which abandons itself to the Supreme Mind finds itself related to all its works and will travel a royal road to particular knowledge and powers." We would do well to think deeply about that statement. Is he not saying that rather than trying to make something happen by our willpower, if we turn our life over, so to speak, to that native intelligence within, if we say yes to what is pressing to express in us, and trust, then things seem to happen like magic. Doors open, the right opportunities appear. What we need to take the next step appears. We could call this living in Grace. That is what Holmes meant when he said we feel as if God were specifying just for us (answering our prayers as soon as we say them). Our trust, our faith, our YES becomes an ongoing "prayer," an affirming consciousness.

Emerson stresses our oneness with the Over-Soul. The unity of all things is a basic tenet of Holmes' Science of Mind. We are not separated from anything! Not God, not Cause, not creative intelligence, not love, not Power, not supply, not possibility. We certainly are not separated from what is trying to happen by means of us. Both of these great minds felt that the descent of Spirit into form was inevitable; rather a natural progression of self-awareness, the impulse to be revealed. Consequently, you and I are that revelation. Our life is meant to reveal what Spirit is; that is the how of "getting our Good." It is the expression of it (like love) that produces images of it in our personal world.

As you read "The Over-Soul," it's important to note perhaps the most powerful statement of this essay: "I the Imperfect adore my own Perfect." Say it slowly to fully understand the transformative power it contains. There is a function of conscious mind that can observe the Self behind the ego. We take our attention into that field through meditation, prayer, contemplation, ritual. What we discover right within ourselves is that Being who has never been damaged or diminished by any experience in the physical realm. It remains forever intact. It is the eternal potential of the individualization of God. We carry it forward through this lifetime and the next and the next. Although Holmes did not teach reincarnation as an established fact, he did believe life never dies, is ongoing and forever becoming "the only begotten."

—Dr. Carol Carnes

The Over-Soul

Ralph Waldo Emerson

"But souls that of his own good life partake,
He loves as his own self; dear as his eye
They are to Him: He'll never them forsake:
When they shall die, then God himself shall die:
They live, they live in blest eternity."

—Henry More

THERE IS A DIFFERENCE between one and another hour of life in their authority and subsequent effect. Our faith comes in moments; our vice is habitual. Yet there is a depth in those brief moments which constrains us to ascribe more reality to them than to all other experiences. For this reason the argument which is always forthcoming to silence those who conceive extraordinary hopes of many, namely the appeal to experience, is forever invalid and vain. We give up the past to the objector, and yet we hope. He must explain this hope. We grant that human life is mean, but how did we find out that it was mean? What is the ground of this uneasiness of ours; of this old discontent? What is the universal sense of want and ignorance, but the fine innuendo by which the soul makes its enormous claim?

Why do people feel that the natural history of human-ity has never been written, but they are always leaving behind what you have said of them, and it becomes old, and books of metaphysics worthless? The philosophy of six thousand years has not searched the chambers and magazines of the soul. In its experiments there has always remained, in the last analysis, a residuum it could not resolve. Human nature is a stream whose source is hidden. Our being is descending into us from we know not whence. The most exact calculator has no prescience that somewhat incalculable may not balk the very next moment. I am constrained every moment to acknowledge a higher origin for events than the will I call mine.

As with events, so is it with thoughts. When I watch that flowing river, which, out of regions I see not, pours for a season its streams into me, I see that I am a pen-sioner; not a cause, but a surprised spectator of this ethereal water; that I desire and look up and put myself in the attitude of reception, but from some alien energy the visions come.

The Supreme Critic on the errors of the past and the present, and the only prophet of that which must be, is that great nature in which we rest as the earth lies in the soft arms of the atmosphere; that Unity, that Over-Soul, within which every person's particular being is contained and made one with all other; that common heart of which all sincere conversation is the worship, to which all right action is submission; that overpowering reality which confutes our tricks and talents, and constrains everyone to pass for what he is, and to speak from his character and not from his tongue, and which evermore tends to pass into our thought and hand and become wisdom and virtue and power and beauty. We live in succession, in division, in parts, in particles. Meantime within us is the soul of the whole; the wise silence; the universal beauty, to which every part and particle is equally related; the eternal ONE. And this deep power in which we exist and whose beatitude is all accessible to us, is not only self-sufficing and perfect in every hour, but the act of seeing and the thing seen, the seer and the spectacle, the subject and the object, are one. We see the world piece by piece, as the sun, the moon, the animal, the tree; but the whole, of which these are the shining parts, is the soul. Only by the vision of that Wisdom can the horoscope of the ages be read, and by falling back on our better thoughts, by yielding to the spirit of prophecy which is innate in every individual, we can know what it saith. The words of one who speaks from that life must sound vain to those who do not dwell in the same thought on their own part. I dare not speak for it. My words do not carry its august sense; they fall short and cold. Only itself can inspire whom it will, and behold! their speech shall be lyrical, and sweet, and universal as the rising of the wind. Yet I desire, even by profane words, if I may not use sacred, to indicate the heaven of this deity and to report what hints I have collected of the transcendent simplicity and energy of the Highest Law.

If we consider what happens in conversation, in reveries, in remorse, in times of passion, in surprises, in the instructions of dreams, wherein often we see ourselves in masquerade—the droll disguises only magnifying and enhancing a real element and forcing it on our distinct notice—we shall catch many hints that will broaden and lighten into knowledge of the secret of nature. All goes to show that the soul within is not an organ, but animates and exercises all the organs; is not a function, like the power of memory, of calculation, of comparison, but uses these as hands and feet; is not a faculty, but a light; is not the intellect or the will, but the master of the intellect and the will; is the background of our being, in which they lie—an immensity not possessed and that cannot be possessed. From within or from behind, a light shines through us upon things and makes us aware that we are nothing, but the light is all. One's physique is the facade of a temple wherein all wisdom and all good abide. What we commonly call a human being, the eating, drinking, planting, counting person, does not, as we know them, represent themselves, but misrepresents themselves. That which we see we do not respect, but the soul, whose organ they are, would they let it appear through their actions, would make our knees bend. When it breathes through their intellect, it is genius; when it breathes through their will, it is virtue; when it flows through their affection, it is love. And the blindness of the intellect begins when it would be something of itself. The weakness of the will begins when the individual would be something of themselves. All reform aims in some one particular to let the soul have its way through us; in other words, to engage us to obey.

Of this pure nature every individual is at some time sensible. Language cannot paint it with his colors. It is too subtle. It is undefinable, unmeasurable; but we know that it pervades and contains us. We know that all spiritual being is in us. A wise old proverb says, "God comes to see us without bell"; that is, as there is no screen or ceiling between our heads and the infinite heavens, so is there no bar or wall in the soul where the physical body, the effect, ceases, and God, the cause, begins. The walls are taken away. We lie open on one side to the deeps of spiritual nature, to the attributes of God. Justice we see and know, Love, Freedom, Power. These natures no one has ever risen above, but they tower over us, and most in the moment when our interests tempt us to wound them.

The sovereignty of this nature whereof we speak is made known by its independency of those limitations which circumscribe us on every hand. The soul circumscribes all things. As I have said, it contradicts all experience. In like manner it abolishes time and space. The influence of the senses has in most people overpowered the mind to that degree that the walls of time and space have come to look real and insurmountable; and to speak with levity of these limits is, in the world, the sign of insanity. Yet time and space are but inverse measures of the force of the soul. The spirit sports with time—"Can crowd eternity into an hour, Or stretch an hour to eternity."

We are often made to feel that there is another youth and age than that which is measured from the year of our natural birth. Some thoughts always find us young, and keep us so. Such a thought is the love of the universal and eternal beauty. Every person parts from that contemplation with the feeling that it rather belongs to ages than to mortal life. The least activity of the intellectual powers redeems us in a degree from the conditions of time. In sickness, in languor, give us a strain of poetry or a profound sentence, and we are refreshed; or produce a volume of Plato or Shakespeare, or remind us of their names, and instantly we come into a feeling of longevity. See how the deep divine thought reduces centuries and millenniums and makes itself present through all ages. Is the teaching of Christ less effective now than it was when first His mouth was opened? The emphasis of facts and persons in my thought has nothing to do with time. And so always the soul's scale is one, the scale of the senses and the understanding is another. Before the revelations of the soul, Time, Space, and Nature shrink away. In common speech we refer all things to time, as we habitually refer the immensely sundered stars to one concave sphere. And so we say that the Judgment is distant or near, that the Millennium approaches, that a day of certain political, moral, social reforms is at hand, and the like, when we mean that in the nature of things one of the facts we contemplate is external and fugitive, and the other is permanent and connate with the soul. The things we now esteem fixed shall, one by one, detach themselves like ripe fruit from our experience, and fall. The wind shall blow them none knows whither. The landscape, the figures, Boston, London, are facts as fugitive as any institution past, or any whiff of mist or smoke, and so is society, and so is the world. The soul looketh steadily forward, creating a world before it, leaving worlds behind. It has no dates, nor rites, nor persons, nor specialties, nor equal. It knows only the soul; the web of events is the flowing robe in which the soul is clothed.

After its own law and not by arithmetic is the rate of its progress to be computed. The soul's advances are not made by gradation, such as can be represented by motion in a straight line, but rather by ascension of state, such as can be represented by metamorphosis—from the egg to the worm, from the worm to the fly. The growths of genius are of a certain total character, that does not advance the elect individual first over John, then Adam, then Richard, and give to each the pain of discovered inferiority—but by every throe of growth one expands there where they work, passing, at each pulsation, classes, populations, of others. With each divine impulse the mind rends the thin rinds of the visible and finite, and comes out into eternity, and inspires and expires its air. It converses with truths that have always been spoken in the world, and becomes conscious of a closer sympathy with Zeno and Arrian than with persons in the house.

This is the law of moral and of mental gain. The simple rise as by specific levity not into a particular virtue, but into the region of all the virtues. They are in the spirit which contains them all. The soul requires purity, but purity is not it; requires justice, but justice is not that; requires beneficence, but is somewhat better;

so that there is a kind of descent and accommodation felt when we leave speaking of moral nature to urge a virtue which it enjoins. To the well-born child all the virtues are natural, and not painfully acquired. Speak to their heart, and the grown child will become suddenly virtuous.

Within the same sentiment is the germ of intellectual growth, which obeys the same law. Those who are capable of humility, of justice, of love, of aspiration stand already on a platform that commands the sciences and arts, speech and poetry, action and grace. For whoso dwells in this moral beatitude already anticipates those special powers which are prized so highly. The lover has no talent, no skill, which passes for quite nothing with their enamoured beloved, however little one may possess of related faculty; and the heart which abandons itself to the Supreme Mind finds itself related to all its works, and will travel a royal road to particular knowledges and powers. In ascending to this primary and aboriginal sentiment we have come from our remote station on the circumference instantaneously to the center of the world, where, as in the closet of God, we see causes, and anticipate the universe, which is but a slow effect.

One mode of the divine teaching is the incarnation of the spirit in a form—in forms, like my own. I live in society, with persons who answer to thoughts in my own mind, or express a certain obedience to the great instincts to which I live. I see its presence to them. I am certified of a common nature; and these other souls, these separated selves, draw me as nothing else can. They stir in me the new emotions we call passion; of love, hatred, fear, admiration, pity; thence come conversation, competition, persuasion, cities, and war. Persons are supplementary to the primary teaching of the soul. In youth we are made for persons. Childhood and youth see all the world in them. But the larger experience beyond youth discovers the identical nature appearing through them all. Persons themselves acquaint us with the impersonal. In all conversation between two persons tacit reference is made, as to a third party, to a common nature. That third party or common nature is not social; it is impersonal; is God. And so in groups where debate is earnest, and especially on high questions, the company become aware that the thought rises to an equal level in all bosoms, that all have a spiritual property in what was said, as well as the sayer. They all become wiser than they were. It arches over them like a temple, this unity of thought in which every heart beats with a nobler sense of power and duty, and thinks and acts with unusual solemnity. All are conscious of attaining to a higher self-possession. It shines for all. There is a certain wisdom of humanity which is common to the greatest men with the lowest, and which our ordinary education often labors to silence and obstruct. The mind is one, and the best minds, who love truth for its own sake, think much less of property in truth. They accept it thankfully everywhere, and do not label or stamp it with any name, for it is theirs long before-hand, and from eternity. The learned and the studious of thought have no monopoly of wisdom. Their vio-lence of direction in some degree disqualifies them to think truly. We owe many valuable observations to peo-ple who are not very acute or profound, and who say the thing without effort which we want and have long been hunting in vain. The action of the soul is oftener in that which is felt and left unsaid than in that which is said in any conversation. It broods over every society, and they unconsciously seek for it in each other. We know better than we do. We do not yet possess our-selves, and we know at the same time that we are much more. I feel the same truth how often in my trivial con-versation with my neighbors, that somewhat higher in each of us overlooks this by-play, and Jove nods to Jove from behind each of us.

There are those who descend to meet. In their habitual and mean service to the world, for which they forsake their native nobleness, they resemble those Arabian sheiks who dwell in mean houses and affect an external poverty, to escape the rapacity of the Pacha, and reserve all their display of wealth for their interior and guarded retirements.

As it is present in all persons, so it is in every period of life. It is adult already in the infant. In my dealing with my child, my Latin and Greek, my accomplishments and my money stead me nothing; but as much soul as I have avails. If I am willful, he sets his will against mine, one for one, and leaves me, if I please, the degradation of beating him by my superiority of strength. But if I renounce my will and act for the soul, setting that up as umpire between us two, out of his young eyes looks the same soul; he reveres and loves with me.

The soul is the perceiver and revealer of truth. We know truth when we see it, let skeptic and scoffer say what they choose. Foolish people ask you, when you have spoken what they do not wish to hear, "How do you know it is truth, and not an error of your own?" We know truth when we see it, from opinion, as we know when we are awake that we are awake. It was a grand sentence of Emanuel Swedenborg, which would alone indicate the greatness of one's perception: "It is no proof of a man's understanding to be able to confirm whatever he pleases; but to be able to discern that what is true is true, and that what is false is false—this is the mark and character of intelligence." In the book I read, the good thought returns to me, as every truth will, the image of the whole soul. To the bad thought which I find in it, the same soul becomes a discerning, separating sword, and lops it away. We are wiser than we know. If we will not interfere with our thought, but will act entirely, or see how the thing stands in God, we know the particular thing, and every thing, and every person. For the Maker of all things and all persons stands behind us and casts their dread omniscience through us over things.

But beyond this recognition of its own in particular passages of the individual's experience, it also reveals truth. And here we should seek to reinforce ourselves by its very presence, and to speak with a worthier, loftier strain of that advent. For the soul's communication of truth is the highest event in nature, since it then does not give somewhat from itself, but it gives itself, or passes into and becomes one with whom it enlightens; or, in proportion to that truth received, it takes that person to itself.

We distinguish the announcements of the soul, its manifestations of its own nature, by the term *Revelation*. These are always attended by the emotion of the sublime. For this communication is an influx of the Divine mind into our mind. It is an ebb of the individual rivulet before the flowing surges of the sea of life. Every distinct apprehension of this central commandment agitates followers with awe and delight. A thrill passes through all at the reception of new truth, or at the performance of a great action, which comes out of the heart of nature. In these communications the power to see is not separated from the will to do, but the insight proceeds from obedience, and the obedience proceeds from a joyful perception. Every moment when the individual feels themselves invaded by it is memorable. By the necessity of our constitution a certain enthusiasm attends the individual's consciousness of that divine presence. The character and duration of this enthusiasm varies with the state of the individual, from an ecstasy and trance and prophetic inspiration—which is its rarer appearance—to the faintest glow of virtuous emotion, in which form it warms, like our household fires, all the families and associations of others, and makes society possible. A certain tendency to insanity has always attended the opening of the religious sense in people, as if they had been "blasted with excess of light." The trances of Socrates, the "union" of Plotinus, the vision of Porphyry, the conversion of Paul, the aurora of Behmen, the convulsions of George Fox and his Quakers, the illumination of Swedenborg, are of this kind. What was in the case of these remarkable persons a ravishment, has, in innumerable instances in common life, been exhibited in less striking manner. Everywhere the history of religion betrays a tendency to enthusiasm. The rapture of the Moravian and Quietist; the opening of the internal sense of the Word, in the language of the New Jerusalem Church; the *revival* of the Calvinistic churches; the *experiences* of the Methodists, are varying forms of that shudder of awe and delight with which the individual soul always mingles with the universal soul.

The nature of these revelations is the same; they are perceptions of the absolute law. They are solutions of the soul's own questions. They do not answer the questions which the understanding asks. The soul answers never by words, but by the thing itself that is inquired after.

Revelation is the disclosure of the soul. The popular notion of a revelation is that it is a telling of fortunes. In past oracles of the soul the understanding seeks to find answers to sensual questions, and undertakes to tell from God how long their lives shall exist, what their hands shall do and who shall be their company, adding names and dates and places. But we must pick no locks. We must check this low curiosity. An answer in words is delusive; it is really no answer to the questions you ask. Do not require a description of the countries towards which you sail. The description does not describe them to you, and tomorrow you arrive there and know them by inhabiting them. Many ask concerning the immortality of the soul, the employments of heaven, the state of the sinner, and so forth. They even dream that Jesus has left replies to precisely these interrogatories. Never a moment did that sublime spirit speak in their *patois*. To truth, justice, love, the attributes of the soul, the idea of immutableness is essentially associated. Jesus, living in these moral sentiments, heedless of sensual fortunes, heeding only the manifestations of these, never made the separation of the idea of duration from the essence of these attributes, nor uttered a syllable concerning the duration of the soul. It was left to His disciples to sever duration from the moral elements, and to teach the immortality of the soul as a doctrine, and maintain it by evidences. The moment the doctrine of the immortality is separately taught, we have already fallen. In the flowing of love, in the adoration of humility, there is no question of continuance. No inspired person ever asks this question or condescends to these evidences. For the soul is true to itself, and the one in whom it is shed abroad cannot wander from the present, which is infinite, to a future which would be finite.

These questions which we lust to ask about the future are a confession of sin. God has no answer for them. No answer in words can reply to a question of things. It is not in an arbitrary "decree of God," but in human nature, that a veil shuts down on the facts of tomorrow; for the soul will not have us read any other cipher than that of cause and effect. By this veil which curtains events it instructs children how to live in today. The only mode of obtaining an answer to these questions of the senses is to forego all low curiosity, and, accepting the tide of being which floats us into the secret of nature, work and live, work and live, and all unawares the advancing soul has built and forged for itself a new condition, and the question and the answer are one.

By the same fire, vital, consecrating, celestial, which burns until it shall dissolve all things into the waves and surges of an ocean of light, we see and know each other, and what spirit each is of. Who can tell the grounds of one's knowledge of the character of the several individuals in their circle of friends? No one. Yet their acts and words do not disappoint them. In that individual, though no ill was known of them, no trust was bestowed. In that other, though they had seldom met, authentic signs had yet passed, to signify that they might be trusted as one who had an interest in their own character. We know each other very well—which of us has been just to themselves and whether that which we teach or behold is only an aspiration or is our honest effort also.

We are all discerners of spirits. That diagnosis lies aloft in our life or unconscious power. The intercourse of society, its trade, its religion, its friendships, its quarrels, is one wide, judicial investigation of character. In full court, or in small committee, or confronted face to face, accuser and accused, people offer themselves to be judged. Against their will they exhibit those decisive trifles by which character is read. But who judges? and what? Not our understanding. We do not read them by learning or craft. No; the wisdom of the wise consists herein, that they do not judge them; they let them judge themselves and merely reads and records their own verdict.

By virtue of this inevitable nature, private will is overpowered, and, maugre our efforts or our imperfections, your genius will speak from you, and mine from me. That which we are, we shall teach, not voluntarily but involuntarily. Thoughts come into our minds by avenues which we never left open, and thoughts go out of our minds through avenues which we never voluntarily opened. Character teaches over our head. The infallible index of true progress is found in the tone one takes. Neither age, nor breeding, nor company, nor books, nor actions, nor talents, nor all together can hinder those from being deferential to a higher spirit than their own. If one has not found a home in God, manners, forms of speech, the turn of sentences, the build, shall I say, of all opinions will involuntarily confess it, let them brave it out how they will. If one has found his center, the Deity will shine through them, through all the disguises of ignorance, of ungenial temperament, of unfavorable circumstance. The tone of seeking is one, and the tone of having is another.

The great distinction between teachers sacred or literary—between poets like Herbert, and poets like Pope—between philosophers like Spinoza, Kant and Coleridge, and philosophers like Locke, Paley, Mackintosh, and Stewart—between people of the world who are reckoned accomplished talkers, and here and there a fervent mystic, prophesying half insane under the infinitude of their thought—is that one class speak *from within*, or from experience, as parties and possessors of the fact; and the other class *from without*, as spectators merely, or perhaps as acquainted with the fact on the evidence of third persons. It is of no use to preach to me from without. I can do that too easily myself. Jesus speaks always from within, and in a degree that transcends all others. In that is the miracle. I believe beforehand that it ought so to be. All stand continually in the expectation of the appearance of such a teacher. But if another does not speak from within the veil, where the word is one with that it tells of, let them lowly confess it.

The same Omniscience flows into the intellect, and makes what we call genius. Much of the wisdom of the world is not wisdom, and the most illuminated class of individuals are no doubt superior to literary fame, and are not writers. Among the multitude of scholars and authors, we feel no hallowing presence; we are sensible of a knack and skill rather than of inspiration; they have a light and know not whence it comes and call it their own; their talent is some exaggerated faculty, some overgrown member, so that their strength is a disease. In these instances the intellectual gifts do not make the impression of virtue, but almost of vice; and we feel that one's talents stand in the way of their advancement in truth. But genius is religious. It is a larger imbibing of the common heart. It is not anomalous, but more like and not less like others. There is in all great poets a wisdom of humanity which is superior to any talents they exercise. The author, the wit, the partisan, the fine citizen, does not take their place. Humanity shines in Homer, in Chaucer, in Spenser, in Shakespeare, in Milton. They are content with truth. They use the positive degree. They seem frigid and phlegmatic to those who have been spiced with the frantic passion and violent coloring of inferior but popular writers. For they are poets by the free course which they allow to the informing soul, which through their eyes beholds again and blesses the things which it hath made. The soul is superior to its knowledge, wiser than any of its works.

The great poet makes us feel our own wealth, and then we think less of their compositions. Their best communication to our mind is to teach us to despise all they have done. Shakespeare carries us to such a lofty strain of intelligent activity as to suggest a wealth which beggars his own; and we then feel that the splendid works which he has created, and which in other hours we extol as a sort of self-existent poetry, take no stronger hold of real nature than the shadow of a passing traveler on the rock. The inspiration which uttered itself in *Hamlet* and *Lear* could utter things as good from day to day forever. Why then should I make account of *Hamlet* and *Lear*, as if we had not the soul from which they fell as syllables from the tongue?

This energy does not descend into individual life on any other condition than entire possession. It comes to the lowly and simple; it comes to whomsoever will put off what is foreign and proud; it comes as insight; it comes as serenity and grandeur. When we see those whom it inhabits, we are apprised of new degrees of greatness. From that inspiration one comes back with a changed tone. They do not talk with others with an eye to their opinion. They try them. It requires of us to be plain and true. The vain traveler attempts to embellish their life by quoting my lord and the prince and the countess, who thus said or did to them. The ambitious vulgar show you their spoons and brooches and rings, and preserve their cards and compliments. The more cultivated, in their account of their own experience, cull out the pleasing, poetic circumstance—the visit to Rome, the great genius they saw; the brilliant friend they know; still further on perhaps the gorgeous landscape, the mountain lights, the mountain thoughts they enjoyed yesterday—and so seek to throw a romantic color over their life. But the soul that ascends to worship the great God is plain and true; has no rose-color, no fine friends, no chivalry, no adventures; does not want admiration; dwells in the hour that now is, in the earnest experience of the common day—by reason of the present moment and the mere trifle having become porous to thought and bibulous of the sea of light.

Converse with a mind that is grandly simple, and literature looks like word-catching. The simplest utterances are worthiest to be written, yet are they so cheap and so things of course, that in the infinite riches of the soul it is like gathering a few pebbles off the ground, or bottling a little air in a phial, when the whole earth and the whole atmosphere are ours. Nothing can pass there, or make you one of the circle, but the casting aside your trappings, and dealing face to face in naked truth, plain confession, and omniscient affirmation.

Souls such as these treat you as gods would, walk as

gods in the earth, accepting without any admiration your wit, your bounty, your virtue even—say rather your act of duty, for your virtue they own as their proper blood, royal as themselves, and over-royal, and the father of the gods. But what rebuke their plain fraternal bearing casts on the mutual flattery with which authors solace each other and wound themselves! These flatter not. I do not wonder that these people go to see Cromwell and Christina and Charles the Second and James the First and the Grand Turk. For they are, in their own elevation, the fellows of kings, and must feel the servile tone of conversation in the world. They must always be a godsend to princes, for they confront them, a king to a king, without ducking or concession, and give a high nature the refreshment and satisfaction of resistance, of plain humanity, of even companionship and of new ideas. They leave them wiser and superior individuals. Souls like these make us feel that sincerity is more excellent than flattery. Deal so plainly with man and woman as to constrain the utmost sincerity and destroy all hope of trifling with you. It is the highest compliment you can pay. Their "highest praising," said Milton, "is not flattery, and their plainest advice is a kind of praising."

Ineffable is our union with God in every act of the soul. The simplest person who in their integrity worships God, becomes God; yet for ever and ever the influx of this better and universal self is new and unsearchable. It inspires awe and astonishment. How dear, how soothing to all, arises the idea of God, peopling the lonely place, effacing the scars of our mistakes and disappointments! When we have broken our god of tradition and ceased from our god of rhetoric, then may God fire the heart with his presence. It is the doubling of the heart itself, nay, the infinite enlargement of the heart with a power of growth to a new infinity on every side. It inspires in us an infallible trust. We have not the conviction, but the sight, that the best is the true, and may in that thought easily dismiss all particular uncertainties and fears, and adjourn to the sure revelation of time the solution of our private riddles. We are sure that our welfare is dear to the heart of being. In the presence of law to our mind we are overflowed with a reliance so universal that it sweeps away all cherished hopes and the most stable projects of mortal condition in its flood. We believe that we cannot escape from our good. The things that are really for thee gravitate to thee. You are running to seek your friend. Let your feet run, but your mind need not. If you do not find them, will you not acquiesce that it is best you should not find them? For there is a power, which, as it is in you, is in them also, and could therefore very well bring you together, if it were for the best. You are preparing with eagerness to go and render a service to which your talent and your taste invite you, the love of others and the hope of fame. Has it not occurred to you that you have no right to go, unless you are equally willing to be prevented from going? O, believe, as thou livest, that every sound that is spoken over the round world, which thou oughtest to hear, will vibrate on thine ear! Every proverb, every book, every byword that belongs to thee for aid or comfort, shall surely come home through open or winding passages. Every friend whom not thy fantastic will but the great and tender heart in thee craveth, shall lock thee in his embrace. And this because the heart in thee is the heart of all; not a valve, not a wall, not an intersection is there anywhere in nature, but one blood rolls uninterruptedly an endless circulation through all, as the water of the globe is all one sea, and, truly seen, its tide is one.

Let one and all then learn the revelation of all nature and all thought to their heart; this, namely; that the Highest dwells with them; that the sources of nature are in their own mind, if the sentiment of duty is there. But if one would know what the great God speaketh, they must "go into their closet and shut the door," as Jesus said. God will not manifest within cowards. They must greatly listen to themselves, withdrawing themselves from all the accents of another's devotion. Even their prayers are hurtful to them, until they have made their own. Our religion vulgarly stands on numbers of believers. Whenever the appeal is made—no matter how indirectly—to numbers, proclamation is then and there made that religion is not. Those that find God a sweet enveloping thought to themselves never count their company. When I sit in that presence, who shall dare to come in? When I rest in perfect humility, when I burn with pure love, what can Calvin or Swedenborg say?

It makes no difference whether the appeal is to numbers or to one. The faith that stands on authority is not faith. The reliance on authority measures the decline of religion, the withdrawal of the soul. The position people have given to Jesus, now for many centuries of history, is a position of authority. It characterizes themselves. It cannot alter the eternal facts. Great is the soul, and plain. It is no flatterer, it is no follower; it never appeals from itself. It believes in itself. Before the immense possibilities of one's life, all mere experience, all past biography, however spotless and sainted, shrinks away. Before that heaven which our presentiments foreshow us, we cannot easily praise any form of life we have seen or read of. We not only affirm that we have few that are great and wise, but, absolutely speaking, that we have none; that we have no history, no record of any character or mode of living that entirely contents us. The saints and demigods whom history worships we are constrained to accept with a grain of allowance. Though in our lonely hours we draw a new strength out of their memory, yet, pressed on our attention, as they are by the thoughtless and customary, they fatigue and invade. The soul gives itself, alone, original and pure, to the Lonely, Original, and Pure, who, on that condition, gladly inhabits, leads, and speaks through it. Then is it glad, young and nimble. It is not wise, but it sees through all things. It is not called religious, but it is innocent. It calls the light its own, and feels that the grass grows and the stone falls by a law inferior to, and dependent on, its nature. Behold, it saith, I am born into the great, the universal mind. I, the imperfect, adore my own Perfect. I am somehow receptive of the great soul, and thereby I do overlook the sun and the stars and feel them to be the fair accidents and effects which change and pass. More and more the surges of everlasting nature enter into me, and I become public and human in my regards and actions. So come I to live in thoughts and act with energies which are immortal. Thus revering the soul, and learning, as the ancient said, that "its beauty is immense," all humanity will come to see that the world is the perennial miracle which the soul worketh, and be less astonished at particular wonders; they will learn that there is no profane history; that all history is sacred; that the universe is represented in an atom, in a moment of time. They will weave no longer a spotted life of shreds and patches, but will live with a divine unity. They will cease from what is base and frivolous in life and be content with all places and with any service they can render. They will calmly front the morrow in the negligency of that trust which carries God with it and so hath already the whole future in the bottom of the heart.

QUESTIONS TO CONSIDER:

1. What does Emerson mean that our vice is habitual and our faith comes in moments?

2. Have you ever had an experience of Oneness or of the Divine Presence?

3. How do we misrepresent ourselves (like the sheik who pretends to be poor, fearing robbers)?

4. Do you feel like you are a sentient being? If so, in what ways?

5. Has your image of "soul" changed in recent years?

6. How do we "abandon ourselves to the Supreme Mind"?

7. "The soul is the perceiver and revealer of Truth." Explain.

8. What does Emerson mean when he says, "God has no answer" about the future?

9. "That which we are, we shall teach, voluntarily or involuntarily." How does this relate to your life?

10. Do you feel a "calling" to do or be something in particular?

Spiritual Laws
Emerson the Cosmologist

OVERVIEW:

THIS IS A SPIRITUAL UNIVERSE GOVERNED BY SPIRITUAL LAWS. THEY ARE OURS TO OBEY, AND THEREFORE OURS TO USE TO OUR ADVANTAGE.

EMERSON KNEW THAT Faith must be rooted in Reality. Religious piety in his view was a false faith, based on institutional thinking. He espoused faith in the unseen principles that govern how things happen. Ernest Holmes taught a similar perception, that we do not accept a "blind faith" but an informed faith. The whole of New Thought is not about why things happen to us (as in why do good things happen to bad people and vice versa) but how does anything come to be? How does an idea become a thing? How does invisible sound become music? How does the not yet known become the known? Emerson and Holmes believed in Spiritual Laws whether we know about them or not.

Holmes writes in *The Science of Mind*, "If we believe that It will not work, in Reality It really works by appearing to 'not work.' When we believe that It cannot and will not, then according to the Principle, It DOES NOT. But when It does not, it still does, only It does according to our belief that It will not. This is our own punishment through the Law of Cause and Effect."

Right there on the first page of this essay Emerson states the great Truth: "The soul will not know either deformity or pain." He is speaking of the individualized soul that is our essential self and the greater soul we refer to as universal or God. Neither knows anything other than pure love and Intelligence, infinite potential and the ever present now.

There is no time or space on the infinite level. What this means to us is that our pain is local. God does not heal or repair. God restores the image and likeness as us, whole and resting in an active potential. Our grief is our perception. Our ill health is an effect of our beliefs, not a cause in and of itself. If this were not true, we could not surpass the past. We would be limited by it and of course we are not. Holmes and Emerson both championed our innate transcendence. We are greater than any experience we have or will ever have or have had.

In Spiritual Laws, Emerson helps us to understand how the very thing we may have lamented earlier actually has served to "launch" us somehow to where we are today. (The essay "Compensation" also goes into greater detail about this.) He speaks of a "deep, remedial force" that underlies all facts. We come to see that what we thought was the worst thing that could have happened turns out to be the most significant turning point in our personal journey. He uses the example of how sailboats move forward, not in a straight line but by twists and turns, catching the wind. Holmes taught something similar in that he believed in One Power, a Power for Good, with no agenda other than to reveal itself by means of its created expression (conscious life). That would be us. Our experience is determined by how conscious we are of the "deep remedial force" as the constant intelligence working to bring about our greater Good. Neither man believed in Kismet or predestination, but both felt our innate Self was destined to thrive.

The deep remedial force can be seen as the Presence functioning as Principle. God as Law is how Holmes would state it; not knowing what it is doing, only that it is compelled to do what we empower it to work with (our consciousness.) "Life alone can impart Life." Our conviction, our passion, our love are the components of authentic expression. Emerson wrote: "The effect of every action is measured by the depth of the sentiment from which it proceeds." While Holmes stressed the hidden principles behind creation, he saw that halfhearted ideas would never materialize or become experiences.

"Human character does evermore publish itself." Here again Emerson is speaking to the necessity of congruency. What we really believe and who we think we are and our perceptions of reality come through no matter how much we may try to convince the world otherwise. "Your silence answers very loudly." Have you ever been in a room full of people when someone new enters? All heads turn to see what it is they felt. The consciousness precedes the form. Always.

In *The Science of Mind*, Holmes places self-identity as the origin of our perceptions, beliefs, emotions, and how we react to the world. Find out, he advised, who you really are. We cannot hide who we think we are for long. "A person passes for what they are worth" (in their own eyes).

Emerson's most famous quote is in this section of the essay. "Be and not seem. Let us acquiesce. Let us take our bloated nothingness out of the path of the divine circuits." Holmes would say our bloated nothingness is our false beliefs, our unwarranted fears, our ego mind, which sees most things as a threat to its existence. Holmes then goes on to say, "Take your attention away from the outer world on a regular basis. Let the thoughts float away. The divine circuits are the 'forever becoming' of God, attempting to come into our life as manifest reality." The Law "takes us at our word." It cannot give us more or less than our self-identity can accept. It is a principle not a person.

Emerson and Holmes had this in common: Both were intellectual giants, interested in the *how* of things. They were also Mystics, feeling the Presence everywhere, seeing it in all things. Perhaps more than most, they were able to "judge not by appearances."

Both men saw God as an indwelling Life Force, a pure Love, and an unchallenged Intelligence. In Emerson's day, the Transcendentalists were considered eccentric and a threat to traditionalists. Indeed, Holmes, in his attempts to liberate religion from superstition and dogma, also walked a tightrope in a Judeo-Christian culture. Both men faced ridicule, and yet, their words were so compelling to those who had ears to hear, thousands became true believers.

At the end of Spiritual Laws, Emerson said, "I desire not to disgrace the soul." He felt there was an aspect to him that he could strive to live up to. He said, "The fact that I am here shows me the soul had need of an organ here. Shall I not assume the post?" That is a good question for us all.

Our five senses serve a purpose, of course, but

they are only superficial perceptions colored by our self-identity and are often incorrect. Shall we trust only our five senses, or shall we turn to the Source within, becoming a co-creator with its Power to make all things new? Think of some time when you were convinced of something because you were sure you saw it correctly, only to discover later that your perception was wrong. It has happened to most of us, and it proves the Truth. We see what we believe is ours to see.

—Dr. Carol Carnes

Spiritual Laws

Ralph Waldo Emerson

The living Heaven thy prayers respect,
House at once and architect,
Quarrying man's rejected hours,
Builds therewith eternal towers;
Sole and self-commanded works,
Fears not undermining days,
Grows by decays,
And, by the famous might that lurks
In reaction and recoil,
Makes flame to freeze, and ice to boil;
Forging, through swart arms of Offence,
The silver seat of Innocence.

WHEN THE ACT OF REFLECTION takes place in the mind, when we look at ourselves in the light of thought, we discover that our life is embosomed in beauty. Behind us, as we go, all things assume pleasing forms, as clouds do far off. Not only things familiar and stale, but even the tragic and terrible are comely as they take their place in the pictures of memory. The river-bank, the weed at the water-side, the old house, the foolish person, however neglected in the passing, have a grace in the past. Even the corpse that has lain in the chambers has added a solemn ornament to the house. The soul will not know either deformity or pain. If in the hours of clear reason we should speak the severest truth, we should say that we had never made a sacrifice. In these hours the mind seems so great that nothing can be taken from us that seems much. All loss, all pain, is particular; the universe remains to the heart unhurt. Neither vexations nor calamities abate our trust. No one ever stated their griefs as lightly as they might. Allow for exaggeration in the most patient and sorely ridden hack that ever was driven. For it is only the finite that has wrought and suffered; the infinite lies stretched in smiling repose.

The intellectual life may be kept clean and healthful if we will live the life of nature and not import into our mind difficulties which are none of ours. No one need be perplexed in their speculations. Let them do and say what strictly belongs to them, and though very ignorant of books, their nature shall not yield them any intellectual obstructions and doubts. Our young people are diseased with the theological problems of original sin, origin of evil, predestination and the like. These never presented a practical difficulty to anyone—never darkened across someone's road who did not go out of their way to seek them. These are the soul's mumps and measles and whooping-coughs, and those who have not caught them cannot describe their health or prescribe the cure. A simple mind will not know these enemies. It is quite another thing that one should be able to give account of their faith and expound to another the theory of his self-union and freedom. This requires rare gifts. Yet without this self-knowledge there may be a sylvan strength and integrity in that which they are. "A few strong instincts and a few plain rules" suffice us.

My will never gave the images in my mind the rank they now take. The regular course of studies, the years of academical and professional education have not yielded me better facts than some idle books under the bench at the Latin School. What we do not call education is more precious than that which we call so. We form no guess, at the time of receiving a thought, of its comparative value. And education often wastes its effort in attempts to thwart and balk this natural magnetism, which is sure to select what belongs to it.

In like manner our moral nature is vitiated by any interference of our will. People represent virtue as a struggle, and take to themselves great airs upon their attainments, and the question is everywhere vexed when a noble nature is commended, whether one is not better who strives with temptation. But there is no merit in the matter. Either God is there or not there. We love characters in proportion as they are impulsive and spontaneous. The less one thinks or knows about their virtues the better we like them. Timoleon's victories are the best victories, which ran and flowed like Homer's verses, Plutarch said. When we see a soul whose acts are all regal, graceful, and pleasant as roses, we must thank God that such things can be and are, and not turn sourly on the angel and say "Crump is a better man with his grunting resistance to all his native devils."

Not less conspicuous is the preponderance of nature over will in all practical life. There is less intention in history than we ascribe to it. We impute deep-laid far-sighted plans to Cæsar and Napoleon; but the best of their power was in nature, not in them. Individuals of an extraordinary success, in their honest moments, have always sung, "Not unto us, not unto us." According to the faith of their times they have built altars to Fortune, or to Destiny, or to St. Julian. Their success lay in their parallelism to the course of thought, which found in them an unobstructed channel; and the wonders of which they were the visible conductors seemed to the eye their deed. Did the wires generate the galvanism? It is even true that there was less in them on which they could reflect than in another; as the virtue of a pipe is to be smooth and hollow. That which externally seemed will and immovableness was willingness and self-annihilation. Could Shakespeare give a theory of Shakespeare?

Could ever those of prodigious mathematical genius convey to others any insight into their methods? If they could communicate that secret it would instantly lose its exaggerated value, blending with the daylight and the vital energy the power to stand and to go.

The lesson is forcibly taught by these observations that our life might be much easier and simpler than we make it; that the world might be a happier place than it is; that there is no need of struggles, convulsions, and despairs, of the wringing of the hands and the gnashing of the teeth; that we miscreate our own evils. We interfere with the optimism of nature; for whenever we get this vantage-ground of the past, or of a wiser mind in the present, we are able to discern that we are begirt with laws which execute themselves.

The face of external nature teaches the same lesson. Nature will not have us fret and fume. Nature does not like our benevolence or our learning much better than it likes our frauds and wars. When we come out of the caucus, or the bank, or the Abolition-convention, or the Temperance-meeting, or the Transcendental club into the fields and woods, Nature says to us, "So hot? my little friend."

We are full of mechanical actions. We must needs intermeddle and have things in our own way, until the sacrifices and virtues of society are odious. Love should make joy; but our benevolence is unhappy. Our Sunday-schools and churches and pauper-societies are yokes to the neck. We pain ourselves to please nobody. There are natural ways of arriving at the same ends at which these aim, but do not arrive. Why should all virtue work in one and the same way? Why should all give dollars? It is very inconvenient to us country folk, and we do not think any good will come of it. We have not dollars; merchants have; let them give them. Farmers will give corn; poets will sing; women will sew; laborers will lend a hand; the children will bring flowers. And why drag this dead weight of a Sunday-school over the whole Christendom? It is natural and beautiful that childhood should inquire and maturity should teach; but it is time enough to answer questions when they are asked. Do not shut up the young people against their will in a pew and force the children to ask them questions for an hour against their will.

If we look wider, things are all alike; laws and letters and creeds and modes of living seem a travesty of truth. Our society is encumbered by ponderous machinery, which resembles the endless aqueducts which the Romans built over hill and dale and which are superseded by the discovery of the law that water rises to the level of its source. It is a Chinese wall which any nimble Tartar can leap over. It is a standing army, not so good as a peace. It is a graduated, titled, richly appointed empire, quite superfluous when town-meetings are found to answer just as well.

Let us draw a lesson from nature, which always works by short ways. When the fruit is ripe, it falls. When the fruit is despatched, the leaf falls. The circuit of the waters is mere falling. The walking of people and all animals is a falling forward. All our manual labor and works of strength, as prying, splitting, digging, rowing and so forth, are done by dint of continual falling, and the globe, earth, moon, comet, sun, star, fall for ever and ever.

The simplicity of the universe is very different from the simplicity of a machine. One who sees moral nature out and out and thoroughly knows how knowledge is acquired and character formed, is a pedant. The simplicity of nature is not that which may easily be read, but is inexhaustible. The last analysis can no wise be made. We judge of an individual's wisdom by their hope, knowing that the perception of the inexhaustibleness of nature is an immortal youth. The wild fertility of nature is felt in comparing our rigid names and reputations with our fluid consciousness. We pass in the world for sects and schools, for erudition and piety, and we are all the time jejune babes. One sees very well how Pyrrhonism grew up. Every person sees that they are that middle point whereof everything may be affirmed and denied with equal reason. One is old, one is young, one is very wise, one is altogether ignorant. They hear and feel what you say of the seraphim, and of the tin-peddler. There is no permanent wise authority except in the figment of the Stoics. We side with the hero, as we read or paint, against the coward and the robber; but we have been ourselves that coward and robber, and shall be again—not in the low circumstance, but in comparison with the grandeurs possible to the soul.

A little consideration of what takes place around us every day would show us that a higher law than that of our will regulates events; that our painful labors are unnecessary and fruitless; that only in our easy, simple, spontaneous action are we strong, and by contenting ourselves with obedience we become divine. Belief and love—a believing love will relieve us of a vast load of care. O my brothers, God exists. There is a soul at the center of nature and over the will of all, so that none of us can wrong the universe. It has so infused its strong enchantment into nature that we prosper when we accept its advice, and when we struggle to wound its creatures our hands are glued to our sides, or they beat our own breasts. The whole course of things goes to teach us faith. We need only obey. There is guidance for each of us, and by lowly listening we shall hear the right word. Why need you choose so painfully your place and occupation and associates and modes of action and of entertainment? Certainly there is a possible right for you that precludes the need of balance and willful election. For you there is a reality, a fit place and congenial duties. Place yourself in the middle of the stream of power and wisdom which animates all whom it floats, and you are without effort impelled to truth, to right and a perfect contentment. Then you put all gainsayers in the wrong. Then you are the world, the measure of right, of truth, of beauty. If we will not be mar-plots with our miserable interferences, the work, the society, letters, arts, science, religion would go on far better than now, and the heaven predicted from the beginning of the world, and still predicted from the bottom of the heart, would organize itself, as do now the rose and the air and the sun.

I say, *do not choose*; but that is a figure of speech by which I would distinguish what is commonly called *choice* among all, and which is a partial act, the choice of the hands, of the eyes, of the appetites, and not a whole act of the individual. But that which I call right or goodness, is the choice of my constitution; and that which I call heaven, and inwardly aspire after, is the state or circumstance desirable to my constitution; and the action which I in all my years tend to do, is the work for my faculties. We must hold a ourselves amenable to reason for the choice of our daily craft or profession. It is not an excuse any longer for our deeds that they are the custom of our trade. What business have we with an evil trade? Have we not a *calling* in his character?

Each person has their own vocation. The talent is the call. There is one direction in which all space is open to them. They have faculties silently inviting them thither to endless exertion. They are like a ship in a river; they run against obstructions on every side but one, on that side all obstruction is taken away and they sweep serenely over a deepening channel into an infinite sea. This talent and this call depend on their organization, or the mode in which the general soul incarnates itself in them. They incline to do something which is easy and good for them when it is done, but which no other can do. They have no rival. For the more truly they consult their own powers, the more difference will their work exhibit from the work of any other. Their ambition is exactly proportioned to their powers. The height of the pinnacle is determined by the breadth of the base. All people have this call of the power to do somewhat unique, and no one has any other call. The pretense that one has another call, a summons by name and personal election and outward "signs that mark them extraordinary, and not in the roll of a commoner," is fanaticism, and betrays obtuseness to perceive that there is one mind in all the individuals, and no respect of persons therein.

By doing one's work they make the need felt which they can supply, and create the taste by which it is enjoyed. They provoke the wants to which they can minister. By doing one's own work they unfold themselves. It is the vice of our public speaking that it has no abandonment. Somewhere, not only every orator but every person should let out all the length of all the reins; should find or make a frank and hearty expression of what force and meaning is in them. The common experience is that we fit ourselves as well as we can to the customary details of that work or trade we fall into, and tend it as a dog turns a spit. Then we are a part of the machine we move; our soul is lost. Until we can manage to communicate ourselves to others in full stature and proportion, we have yet to find our vocation. We must find in that an outlet for our character, so that we may justify our work to their eyes. If the labor is mean, let us by our thinking and character make it liberal. Whatever we know and think, whatever in our apprehension is worth doing, that let us communicate, or we will never be known and honored aright. Foolish, whenever you take the meanness and formality of that thing you do, instead of converting it into the obedient spiracle of your character and aims.

We like only such actions as have already long had the praise of all others, and do not perceive that anything one can do may be divinely done. We think greatness entailed or organized in some places or duties, in certain offices or occasions, and do not see that Paganini can extract rapture from a catgut, and Eulenstein from a jews-harp, and a nimble-fingered lad out of shreds of paper with his scissors, and Landseer out of swine, and the hero out of the pitiful habitation and company in which he was hidden. What we call obscure condition or vulgar society is that condition and society whose poetry is not yet written, but which you shall presently make as enviable and renowned as any. In our estimates let us take a lesson from kings. The parts of hospitality, the connection of families, the impressiveness of death, and a thousand other things, royalty makes its own estimate of, and a royal mind will. To make habitually a new estimate—that is elevation.

What one does, that they have. What have they to do with hope or fear? In themselves is their might. Let them regard no good as solid but that which is in their nature and which must grow out of them as long as they exist. The goods of fortune may come and go like summer leaves; let them scatter the leaves on every wind as the momentary signs of their infinite productiveness.

One may have one's own. Their genius, the quality that differences them from every other, the susceptibility to one class of influences, the selection of what is fit for them, the rejection of what is unfit, determines for them the character of the universe. Each person is a method, a progressive arrangement; a selecting principle, gathering others to themselves wherever they go. They take only their own out of the multiplicity that sweeps and circles round them. They are like one of those booms which are set out from the shore on rivers to catch drift-wood, or like the loadstone amongst splinters of steel. Those facts, words, persons, which dwell in their memory without them being able to say why, remain because they have a relation to them not less real for being as yet unapprehended. They are symbols of value to themselves as they can interpret parts of his consciousness which he would vainly seek words for in the conventional images of books and other minds. What attracts my attention shall have it, as I will go to those who knock at my door, whilst a thousand persons as worthy go by it, to whom I give no regard. It is enough that these particulars speak to me. A few anecdotes, a few traits of character, manners, face, a few incidents, have an emphasis in your memory out of all proportion to their apparent significance if you measure them by the ordinary standards. They relate to your gift. Let them have their weight, and do not reject them and cast about for illustration and facts more usual in literature. What your heart thinks great is great. The soul's emphasis is always right.

Over all things that are agreeable to one's nature and genius, the individual has the highest right. Everywhere they may take what belongs to their spiritual estate, nor can they take anything else though all doors were open, nor can all the force of others hinder one from taking so much. It is vain to attempt to keep a secret from one who has a right to know it. It will tell itself. That mood into which a friend can bring us is their dominion over us. To the thoughts of that state of mind they have a right. All the secrets of that state of mind they can compel. This is a law which political leaders use in practice. All the terrors of the French Republic, which held Austria in awe, were unable to command another's diplomacy. But Napoleon sent to Vienna M. de Narbonne, one of the old noblesse, with the morals, manners, and name of that interest, saying that it was indispensable to send to the old aristocracy of Europe others of the same connection, which, in fact, constitutes a sort of free-masonry. M. de Narbonne in less than a fortnight penetrated all the secrets of the imperial cabinet.

Nothing seems so easy as to speak and to be understood. Yet one may come to find *that* the strongest of defenses and of ties—that they have been understood; and they who have received an opinion may come to find it the most inconvenient of bonds.

If teachers have any opinion which they wish to conceal, their pupils will become as fully indoctrinated into that as into any which they publish. If you pour water into a vessel twisted into coils and angles, it is vain to say, I will pour it only into this or that—it will find its level in all. Others feel and act the consequences of your doctrine without being able to show how they follow. Show us an arc of the curve, and a good mathematician will find out the whole figure. We are always reasoning from the seen to the unseen. Hence the perfect intelligence that subsists between wise thinkers of remote ages. One cannot bury their meanings so deep in a book but time and others of like-mind will find them. Plato had a secret doctrine, had he? What secret can he conceal from the eyes of Bacon? of Montaigne? of Kant? Therefore, Aristotle said of his works, "They are published and not published."

No person can learn what they have not preparation for learning, however near to his eyes is the object. A chemist may tell his most precious secrets to a carpenter, and he shall be never the wiser—the secrets he would not utter to a chemist for an estate. God screens us evermore from premature ideas. Our eyes are holden that we cannot see things that stare us in the face, until the hour arrives when the mind is ripened; then we behold them, and the time when we saw them not is like a dream.

Not in nature but in the individual is all the beauty and worth that can be seen. The world is very empty, and is indebted to this gilding, exalting soul for all its pride. "Earth fills her lap with splendors" *not* her own. The vale of Tempe, Tivoli, and Rome are earth and water, rocks and sky. There are as good earth and water in a thousand places, yet how unaffecting!

People are not the better for the sun and moon, the horizon and the trees; as it is not observed that the keepers of Roman galleries or the valets of painters have any elevation of thought, or that librarians are wiser than others. There are graces in the demeanor of a polished and noble person which are lost upon the eye of a churl. These are like the stars whose light has not yet reached us.

One may see what one maketh. Our dreams are the sequel of our waking knowledge. The visions of the night bear some proportion to the visions of the day. Hideous dreams are exaggerations of the sins of the day. We see our evil affections embodied in bad physiognomies. On the Alps the traveller sometimes beholds their own shadow magnified to a giant, so that every gesture of hand is terrific. "My children," said an old man to his boys scared by a figure in the dark entry, "my children, you will never see anything worse than yourselves." As in dreams, so in the scarcely less fluid events of the world everyone sees themselves in colossal, without knowing that it is themselves. The good, compared to the evil which they see, is as their own good to their own evil. Every quality of their mind is magnified in some one acquaintance, and every emotion of their heart in some one. They are like a quincunx of trees, which counts five—east, west, north, or south; or an initial, medial, and terminal acrostic. And why not? They cleave to one person and avoid another, according to their likeness or unlikeness, truly seeking themselves in their associates and moreover in their trade and habits and gestures and meats and drinks, and comes at last to be faithfully represented by every view you take of their circumstances.

One may read what one writes. What can we see or acquire but what we are? You have observed a skillful person reading Virgil. Well, that author is a thousand books to a thousand persons. Take the book into your two hands and read your eyes out, you will never find what I find. If any ingenious reader would have a monopoly of the wisdom or delight they get, they are as secure now the book is Englished, as if it were imprisoned in the Pelews' tongue. It is with a good book as it is with good company. Introduce a base person among the educated, it is all to no purpose; they are not their fellow. Every society protects itself. The company is perfectly safe, and they are not one of them, though their body is in the room.

What avails it to fight with the eternal laws of mind, which adjust the relation of all persons to each other by the mathematical measure of their havings and beings? Gertrude is enamored of Guy; how high, how aristocratic, how Roman his mien and manners! To live with him were life indeed, and no purchase is too great; and heaven and earth are moved to that end. Well, Gertrude has Guy; but what now avails how high, how aristocratic, how Roman his mien and manners, if his heart and aims are in the senate, in the theatre, and in the billiard-room, and she has no aims, no conversation that can enchant her graceful lord?

One shall have one's own society. We can love nothing but nature. The most wonderful talents, the most meritorious exertions really avail very little with us; but nearness or likeness of nature—how beautiful is the ease of its victory! Persons approach us, famous for their beauty, for their accomplishments, worthy of all wonder for their charms and gifts; they dedicate their whole skill to the hour and the company—with very imperfect result. To be sure it would be ungrateful in us not to praise them loudly. Then, when all is done, a person of related mind, a brother or sister by nature, comes to us so softly and easily, so nearly and intimately, as if it were the blood in our proper veins, that we feel as if some one was gone, instead of another having come; we are utterly relieved and refreshed; it is a sort of joyful solitude. We foolishly think in our days of sin that we must court friends by compliance to the customs of society, to its dress, its breeding, and its estimates. But only that soul can be my friend which I encounter on the line of my own march, that soul to which I do not decline and which does not decline to me, but, native of the same celestial latitude, repeats in its own all my experience. The scholar forgets himself and apes the customs and costumes of the man of the world to deserve the smile of beauty, and follows some giddy girl, not yet taught by religious passion to know the noble woman with all that is serene, oracular, and beautiful in her soul. Let them be great, and love shall follow them. Nothing is more deeply punished than the neglect of the affinities by which alone society should be formed, and the insane levity of choosing associates by others' eyes.

One may set one's own rate. It is a maxim worthy

of all acceptation that people may have that allowance they take. Take the place and attitude which belong to you, and all people acquiesce. The world must be just. It leaves every person, with profound unconcern, to set their own rate. Hero or driveller, it meddles not in the matter. It will certainly accept your own measure of your doing and being, whether you sneak about and deny your own name, or whether you see your work produced to the concave sphere of the heavens, one with the revolution of the stars.

The same reality pervades all teaching. An individual may teach by doing, and not otherwise. If they can communicate themselves they can teach, but not by words. One teaches who gives, and one learns who receives. There is no teaching until the pupil is brought into the same state or principle in which you are; a transfusion takes place; the teacher is you and you are the teacher; then is a teaching, and by no unfriendly chance or bad company can the teacher ever quite lose the benefit. But your propositions run out of one ear as they ran in at the other. We see it advertised that Mr. Grand will deliver an oration on the Fourth of July, and Mr. Hand before the Mechanics' Association, and we do not go thither, because we know that these gentlemen will not communicate their own character and experience to the company. If we had reason to expect such a confidence we should go through all inconvenience and opposition. The sick would be carried in litters. But a public oration is an escapade, a non-committal, an apology, a gag, and not a communication, not a speech, not a speaker.

A like Nemesis presides over all intellectual works. We have yet to learn that the thing uttered in words is not therefore affirmed. It must affirm itself, or no forms of grammar and no plausibility can give it evidence and no array of arguments. The sentence must also contain its own apology for being spoken.

The effect of any writing on the public mind is mathematically measurable by its depth of thought. How much water does it draw? If it awaken you to think, if it lift you from your feet with the great voice of eloquence, then the effect is to be wide, slow, permanent, over the minds of all; if the pages instruct you not, they will die like flies in the hour. The way to speak and write what shall not go out of fashion is to speak and write sincerely. The argument which has not power to reach my own practice, I may well doubt will fail to reach yours. But take Sidney's maxim: "Look in thy heart, and write." Those that write to themselves write to an eternal public. That statement only is fit to be made public which you have come at in attempting to satisfy your own curiosity. The writer who takes a subject from their ear and not from their heart, should know that they have lost as much as they seem to have gained, and when the empty book has gathered all its praise, and half the people say, "What poetry! what genius!" it still needs fuel to make fire. That only profits which is profitable. Life alone can impart life; and though we should burst we can only be valued as we make ourselves valuable. There is no luck in literary reputation. They who make up the final verdict upon every book are not the partial and noisy readers of the hour when it appears, but a court as of angels, a public not to be bribed, not to be entreated and not to be overawed, decides upon one's title to fame. Only those books come down which deserve to last. Gilt edges, vellum and morocco, and presentation-copies to all the libraries will not preserve a book in circulation beyond its intrinsic date. It must go with all Walpole's Noble and Royal Authors to its fate. Blackmore, Kotzebue, or Pollok may endure for a night, but Moses and Homer stand for ever. There are not in the world at any one time more than a dozen persons who read and understand Plato—never enough to pay for an edition of his works; yet to every generation these come duly down, for the sake of those few persons, as if God brought them by hand. "No book," said Bentley, "was ever written down by any but itself." The permanence of all books is fixed by no effort, friendly or hostile, but by their own specific gravity, or the intrinsic importance of their contents to the constant mind of all. "Do not trouble yourself too much about the light on your statue," said Michelangelo to the young sculptor; "the light of the public square will test its value."

In like manner the effect of every action is measured by the depth of the sentiment from which it proceeds. The great ones knew not that they were great. It took a century or two for that fact to appear. What they did, they did because they must; it was the most natural thing in the world, and grew out of the circumstances of the moment. But now, everything they did, even to the lifting of their finger or the eating of bread, looks large, all-related, and is called an institution.

These are the demonstrations in a few particulars of the genius of nature; they show the direction of the stream. But the stream is blood; every drop is alive. Truth has not single victories; all things are its organs— not only dust and stones, but errors and lies. The laws of disease, physicians say, are as beautiful as the laws of health. Our philosophy is affirmative and readily accepts the testimony of negative facts, as every shadow points to the sun. By a divine necessity every fact in nature is constrained to offer its testimony.

Human character evermore publishes itself. The most fugitive deed and word, the mere air of doing a thing, the intimated purpose, expresses character. If you act you show character; if you sit still, if you sleep, you show it. You think because you have spoken nothing when others spoke, and have given no opinion on the times, on the church, on slavery, on marriage, on socialism, on secret societies, on the college, on parties and persons, that your verdict is still expected with curiosity as a reserved wisdom. Far otherwise; your silence answers very loud. You have no oracle to utter, all others have learned that you cannot help them; for oracles speak. Doth not Wisdom cry and Understanding put forth its voice?

Dreadful limits are set in nature to the powers of dissimulation. Truth tyrannizes over the unwilling members of the body. Faces never lie, it is said. No one need be deceived who will study the changes of expression. When an individual speaks the truth in the spirit of truth, their eye is as clear as the heavens. When they have base ends and speak falsely, the eye is muddy and sometimes asquint.

I have heard an experienced counsellor say that he never feared the effect upon a jury of a lawyer who does not believe in his heart that his client ought to have a verdict. If he does not believe it his unbelief will appear to the jury, despite all his protestations, and will become their unbelief. This is that law whereby a work of art, of whatever kind, sets us in the same state of mind wherein the artist was when they made it. That which we do not believe we cannot adequately say, though we may repeat the words never so often. It was this conviction which Swedenborg expressed when he described a group of persons in the spiritual world endeavoring in vain to articulate a proposition which they did not believe; but they could not, though they twisted and folded their lips even to indignation.

One passes for that which one is worth. Very idle is all curiosity concerning other people's estimate of us, and all fear of remaining unknown is not less so. If one knows that they can do anything—that they can do it better than anyone else—they have a pledge of the acknowledgment of that fact by all persons. The world is full of judgment-days, and into every assembly that one enters, in every action they attempt, they are gauged and stamped. In every troop of boys that whoop and run in each yard and square, a new-comer is as well and accurately weighed in the course of a few days and stamped with his right number, as if he had undergone a formal trial of his strength, speed, and temper. A stranger comes from a distant school, with better dress, with trinkets in his pockets, with airs and pretensions; an older boy says to himself, "It's of no use; we shall find him out tomorrow." What has he done? is the divine question which searches us and transpierces every false reputation. A fop may sit in any chair of the world nor be distinguished for his hour from Homer and Washington; but there need never be any doubt concerning the respective ability of human beings. Pretension may sit still, but cannot act. Pretension never feigned an act of real greatness. Pretension never wrote an Iliad, nor drove back Xerxes, nor Christianized the world, nor abolished slavery.

As much virtue as there is, so much appears; as much goodness as there is, so much reverence it commands. All the devils respect virtue. The high, the generous, the self-devoted sect will always instruct and command mankind. Never was a sincere word utterly lost. Never a magnanimity fell to the ground, but there is some heart to greet and accept it unexpectedly. One passes for that which one is worth. What they are engraves itself on their face, on their form, on their fortunes, in letters of light. Concealment avails them nothing, boasting nothing. There is confession in the glances of our eyes, in our smiles, in salutations, and the grasp of hands. Their sin bedaubs them, mars all their good impression. Others know not why they do not trust them, but they do not trust them. Their vice glasses their eye, cuts lines of mean expression in their cheek, pinches the nose, sets the mark of the beast on the back of the head, and writes O fool! fool! on the forehead of a king.

If you would not be known to do anything, never do it. One may play the fool in the drifts of a desert, but every grain of sand shall seem to see. They may be a solitary eater, but cannot keep their foolish counsel. A broken complexion, a swinish look, ungenerous acts and the want of due knowledge—all blab. Can a cook, a Chiffinch, an Iachimo be mistaken for Zeno or Paul? Confucius exclaimed, "How can a man be concealed? How can a man be concealed?"

On the other hand, the hero fears not that if they withhold the avowal of a just and brave act it will go unwitnessed and unloved. One knows it—themselves— and is pledged by it to sweetness of peace and to noble- ness of aim which will prove in the end a better proc- lamation of it than the relating of the incident. Virtue is the adherence in action to the nature of things, and the nature of things makes it prevalent. It consists in a perpetual substitution of being for seeming, and with sublime propriety God is described as saying, I AM.

The lesson which these observations convey is, Be, and not seem. Let us acquiesce. Let us take our bloated nothingness out of the path of the divine circuits. Let us unlearn our wisdom of the world. Let us lie low in the Lord's power and learn that truth alone makes rich and great.

If you visit your friend, why need you apologize for not having visited sooner, and waste their time and deface your own act? Visit them now. Let them feel that the highest love has come to see them, in thee its lowest organ. Or why need you torment yourself and friend by secret self-reproaches that you have not assisted them or complimented them with gifts and salutations heretofore? Be a gift and a benediction. Shine with real light and not with the borrowed reflection of gifts. Those of common standing are apologies for those of greater repute; they bow the head, excuse themselves with prolix reasons, and accumulate appearances because the substance is not.

We are full of these superstitions of sense, the worship of magnitude. We call the poet inactive, because he is not a president, a merchant, or a porter. We adore an institution, and do not see that it is founded on a thought which we have. But real action is in silent moments. The epochs of our life are not in the visible facts of our choice of a calling, our marriage, our acquisition of an office, and the like, but in a silent thought by the way-side as we walk; in a thought which revises our entire manner of life and says, "Thus hast thou done, but it were better thus." And all our after years, like menials, serve and wait on this, and according to their ability execute its will. This revisal or correction is a constant force, which, as a tendency, reaches through our lifetime. The object of all people, the aim of these moments, is to make daylight shine through them, to suffer the law to traverse their whole being without obstruction, so that on what point soever of their doing your eye falls it shall report truly of their character, whether it be their diet, house, religious forms, society, mirth, vote, or their opposition. Now they are not homogeneous, but heterogeneous, and the ray does not traverse; there are no thorough lights, but the eye of the beholder is puzzled, detecting many unlike tendencies and a life not yet at one.

Why should we make it a point with our false modesty to disparage that person we are and that form of being assigned to us? A good person is contented. I love and honor Epaminondas, but I do not wish to be Epaminondas. I hold it more just to love the world of this hour than the world of his hour. Nor can you, if I am true, excite me to the least uneasiness by saying, "He acted and thou sittest still." I see action to be good, when the need is, and sitting still to be also good. Epaminondas, if he was the man I take him for, would have sat still with joy and peace, if his lot had been mine. Heaven is large, and affords space for all modes of love and fortitude. Why should we be busybodies and superserviceable? Action and inaction are alike to the true. One piece of the tree is cut for a weathercock and one for the sleeper of a bridge; the virtue of the wood is apparent in both.

I desire not to disgrace the soul. The fact that I am here certainly shows me that the soul had need of an organ here. Shall I not assume the post? Shall I skulk and dodge and duck with my unseasonable apologies and vain modesty and imagine my being here impertinent? Less pertinent than Epaminondas or Homer being there? And that the soul did not know its own needs? Besides, without any reasoning on the matter, I have no discontent. The good soul nourishes me and unlocks new magazines of power and enjoyment to me every day. I will not meanly decline the immensity of good, because I have heard that it has come to others in another shape.

Besides, why should we be cowed by the name of Action? 'Tis a trick of the senses—no more. We know that the ancestor of every action is a thought. The poor mind does not seem to itself to be any thing unless it have an outside badge—some Gentoo diet, or Quaker coat, or Calvinistic prayer-meeting, or philanthropic society, or a great donation, or a high office, or, anyhow, some wild contrasting action to testify that it is somewhat. The rich mind lies in the sun and sleeps, and is

Nature. To think is to act.

Let us, if we must have great actions, make our own so. All action is of an infinite elasticity, and the least admits of being inflated with the celestial air until it eclipses the sun and moon. Let us seek one peace by fidelity. Let me heed my duties. Why need I go gadding into the scenes and philosophy of Greek and Italian history before I have justified myself to my benefactors? How dare I read Washington's campaigns when I have not answered the letters of my own correspondents? Is not that a just objection to much of our reading? It is a pusillanimous desertion of our work to gaze after our neighbors. It is peeping. Byron says of Jack Bunting, "He knew not what to say, and so he swore."

I may say it of our preposterous use of books—some know not what to do, and so *they read*. I can think of nothing to fill my time with, and I find the Life of Brant. It is a very extravagant compliment to pay to Brant, or to General Schuyler, or to General Washington. My time should be as good as their time—my facts, my net of relations, as good as theirs, or either of theirs. Rather let me do my work so well that other idlers if they choose may compare my texture with the texture of these and find it identical with the best.

This over-estimate of the possibilities of Paul and Pericles, this under-estimate of our own, comes from a neglect of the fact of an identical nature. Bonaparte knew but one merit, and rewarded in one and the same way the good soldier, the good astronomer, the good poet, the good player. The poet uses the names of Cæsar, of Tamerlane, of Bonduca, of Belisarius; the painter uses the conventional story of the Virgin Mary, of Paul, of Peter. The creator does not therefore defer to the nature of these accidental figures in history, of these stock heroes. If the poet writes a true drama, then they are Cæsar, and not the player of Cæsar; then the selfsame strain of thought, emotion as pure, wit as subtle, motions as swift, mounting, extravagant, and a heart as great, self-sufficing, dauntless, which on the waves of its love and hope can uplift all that is reckoned solid and precious in the world—palaces, gardens, money, navies, kingdoms—marking its own incomparable worth by the slight it casts on these gauds of humanity; these all are the poet's, and by the power of these nations are roused. Let a soul believe in God, and not in names and places and persons. Let the great soul incarnated in some woman's form, poor and sad and single, in some Dolly or Joan, go out to service, and sweep chambers and scour floors, and its effulgent daybeams cannot be muffled or hid, but to sweep and scour will instantly appear supreme and beautiful actions, the top and radiance of human life, and all people will get mops and brooms; until, lo! suddenly the great soul has enshrined itself in some other form and done some other deed, and that is now the flower and head of all living nature.

We are the photometers, we the irritable goldleaf and tinfoil that measure the accumulations of the subtle element. We know the authentic effects of the true fire through every one of its million disguises.

QUESTIONS TO CONSIDER:

1. What is the distinction between blind faith and an informed faith?

2. How does "Human character evermore publish itself"?

3. What does Emerson mean by "The soul's emphasis is always right"?

4. Have you felt a "calling" in yourself? Did you follow it? If yes, did you feel at peace and unrestrained?

5. Emerson wrote: "There is a direction in which all space is open to us." Have you had such an experience?

6. How do you feel when Emerson calls out our "bloated nothingness"?

7. What is your current self-identity?

8. What does "If the soul had need of an organ here," mean to you?

9. What is the overriding Spiritual Law Emerson refers to in this essay?

10. Can you see the Law working in your life?

Compensation
Emerson the Accountant

Overview:

THE ESSAY "COMPENSATION" BRINGS THE UNITY
OF ALL THINGS INTO A REALITY LARGER THAN
OUR BEING "ONE WITH EVERYTHING." IT IS
ABOUT HOW IT ALL COMES AROUND AGAIN. THE
IMAGE IS OF THE SERPENT EATING ITS OWN TAIL.
IT IS A PREAMBLE OF SORTS TO "CIRCLES."

EMERSON MAY NOT HAVE KNOWN what a hologram
is, but he describes it perfectly in the beginning of
this essay: "The entire system of things gets represented
in every particle." Quantum physics might say the wave
is in the particle, the particle is in the wave. Spirituality
would state it this way: God is in everything, everything
is in God. More than that, Emerson builds the case for
how Life, in its Infinite Intelligence, balances everything.
When he says, "The barren soil does not breed fevers,
crocodiles, tigers, or scorpions," it is a subtle reference

to the "gift" in every circumstance. Life compensates, keeping everything in balance.

The underlying message is both profound and practically applied. Emerson asserts that nothing is unnoticed by the universe. Our acts will activate a reaction. "Every excess causes a defect, every defect an excess." We often hear humans cry, "It's not fair!" Life is not fair, it is Just.

Human expressions have a way of producing after their own kind, sometimes looking like the very opposite thing. But Life compensates. You steal, you will lose. You give, you will receive. A good image is that of trying to throw away a boomerang by sailing it into the air. It will come right back at us. The idea of this for that is much larger than it seems at first glance. There is no time involved, for it might take a lifetime to get the return on our investment. But return it will. The Hindus with their belief in karma would suggest it might take a few lifetimes for our good to be returned. The point being, we can never lose anything or get away with anything that depletes the general good. It is not punishment but cause/effect on a grand scale.

Emerson states, "If riches increase, they are increased in those that use them." Here is a concrete example of how our participation in the circulation of natural resources (love, joy, peace, supply, creativity, vitality) ensures the growth of them in us. The more we give, the more we have to give. We cannot lose love. Give it to someone and it is stronger in us. All this is simply another way of saying, We cannot outgive God!

Do you remember the old saying, "Do not hold too much good in your hand?" That is the meaning of how the hoarding of anything is a sign of a Lack consciousness. Lack is a lie and when we live from a lie, we will be fearful and stingy, both of which are harmful to our health and well-being. Stinginess often results in physical blockages. The energy is not moving as it should. Compensation is always at work. Balance, balance, balance, Nature cries.

Emerson speaks about how the achievement of Power (as in gaining the White House) costs the person his/her peace. The office itself is tremendously challenging. "Things refuse to be mismanaged for long." We see that truth in our own lifetime with how the mismanagement of our environment has created a threat to humanity itself. Thus, we seek answers to making things right. Again, God as Intelligence is in us: "The universe is represented in every one of its particles." Think the new thought and you will do the new thing. We, by the right use of our native Intelligence shall overcome our own mistakes. This is also true for us personally! "Justice is not postponed." In every essay Emerson teaches that basic truth: Cause/effect are one thing. There is that "deep remedial force" he wrote about in "The Over-Soul," forever involved with human experience, keeping things on an even keel. That may look like earthquakes, hurricanes, floods, and even plague, but there will be an underlying rightness about it. It is the rare person who can see it, but something is being born all the time. It is not that God punishes us, Law demands payment for our acts. There have been Mystics, like Paramahansa Yogananda, who profess the belief that our collective turbulence, our shared unrest, our hates and fears, actually cause the deviations in weather that destroy everything in their path. That would be Compensation in the external world.

Emerson writes again of how we may not see our retribution until after many years. What, at the time, we thought of as the worst thing that could have happened, turns out to be the most significant event in our life. We see the tributaries of the river of effect set in motion by the first act. For example, if we had not been in that collision we would not have had to seek medical help where we met a wonderful person who became very important to us later. Nothing is meaningless, nothing is lost, nothing is taken.

Every loss is a perception that we are less than we were. Emerson reiterates: The whole is in every particle. We cannot be made less than whole, no matter if our body loses limbs, the Self is intact!

Ernest Holmes in *The Science of Mind* underscores our wholeness again and again. Our perception of Self, who we know ourselves to be, is everything. Are we spiritual Beings or not? Is our Source present in us or not? Can we prove to ourselves that our Being is greater than our doing? Yes, we can and must.

Holmes, like Emerson, would have us "sit at home with Cause." In their own way, both espoused that if we do not raise our perception, we are bound by the Law to repeat the patterns we have set in motion. We may heal the body part that was effected, but the dis-ease will find another outlet, perhaps our supply chain or our relationships. Self-identity is paramount in what we know as healing.

In Science of Mind we would assert "we cannot receive more or less than the most dominant of our beliefs." Consciousness precedes form and experience. It is done to us as we believe. Emerson: "Thou shalt be paid exactly for what thou hast done, no more, no less." "Always pay," said Emerson, "for first and last you must pay your entire debt. For every benefit you receive, a tax is levied. He is great who confers the most benefits." He warns us against receiving and not giving in return. Not as a superstition, but as a conscious participant in the circulation of energy that keeps life alive. "Love and you shall be loved."

When I teach from this essay I always suggest to the student that they become very familiar with the last full paragraph of the essay. It is a statement of such profound insight and so exquisitely spoken, that it could serve to remind us of how much we are supported by the universe. Read it out loud again and again.

—Dr. Carol Carnes

Compensation

Ralph Waldo Emerson

EVER SINCE I WAS A BOY I have wished to write a discourse on Compensation; for it seemed to me when very young that on this subject life was ahead of theology and the people knew more than the preachers taught. The documents too from which the doctrine is to be drawn, charmed my fancy by their endless variety, and lay always before me, even in sleep; for they are the tools in our hands, the bread in our basket, the transactions of the street, the farm and the dwelling-house; greetings, relations, debts and credits, the influence of character, the nature and endowment of all. It seemed to me also that in it might be shown a ray of divinity, the present action of the soul of this world, clean from all vestige of tradition; and so the heart might be bathed by an inundation of eternal love, conversing with that which was always known and always must be, because it really is now. It appeared moreover that if this doctrine could be stated in terms with any resemblance to those bright intuitions in which this truth is sometimes revealed to us, it would be a star in many dark hours and crooked passages in our journey, that would not suffer us to lose our way.

I was lately confirmed in these desires by hearing a sermon at church. The preacher, a man esteemed for his orthodoxy, unfolded in the ordinary manner the doctrine of the Last Judgment. He assumed that judgment is not executed in this world; that the wicked are successful; that the good are miserable; and then urged from reason and from Scripture a compensation to be made to both parties in the next life. No offense appeared to be taken by the congregation at this doctrine. As far as I could observe when the meeting broke up they separated without remark on the sermon.

Yet what was the import of this teaching? What did the preacher mean by saying that the good are miserable in the present life? Was it that houses and lands, offices, wine, horses, dress, luxury, are had by the unprincipled, whilst the saints are poor and despised; and that a compensation is to be made to these last hereafter, by giving them the like gratifications another day—bank-stock and doubloons, venison and champagne? This must be the compensation intended; for what else? Is it that they are to have leave to pray and praise? to love and serve others? Why, that they can do now. The legitimate inference the disciple would draw was—"We are to have *such* a good time as the sinners have now"—or, to push it to its extreme import—"You sin now; we shall sin by and by; we would sin now, if we could; not being successful, we expect our revenge tomorrow."

The fallacy lay in the immense concession that the bad are successful; that justice is not done now. The blindness of the preacher consisted in deferring to the base estimate of the market of what constitutes a courageous success, instead of confronting and convicting the world from the truth; announcing the presence of the soul; the omnipotence of the will; and so establishing the standard of good and ill, of success and falsehood.

I find a similar base tone in the popular religious works of the day and the same doctrines assumed by the literary thinkers when occasionally they treat the related topics. I think that our popular theology has gained in decorum, and not in principle, over the superstitions it has displaced. But they are better than their theology. Their daily life gives it the lie. Every ingenuous and aspiring soul leaves the doctrine behind in their own experience, and all feel sometimes the falsehood which they cannot demonstrate. For they are wiser than they know. That which they hear in schools and pulpits without afterthought, if said in conversation would probably be questioned in silence. If one were to dogmatize in a mixed company on Providence and the divine laws, they are answered by a silence which conveys well enough to an observer the dissatisfaction of the hearer, but their incapacity to make their own statement.

I shall attempt in this and the following chapter to record some facts that indicate the path of the law of Compensation; happy beyond my expectation if I shall truly draw the smallest arc of this circle.

Polarity, or action and reaction, we meet in every part of nature; in darkness and light; in heat and cold; in the ebb and flow of waters; in male and female; in the inspiration and expiration of plants and animals; in the equation of quantity and quality in the fluids of the animal body; in the systole and diastole of the heart; in the undulations of fluids, and of sound; in the centrifugal and centripetal gravity; in electricity, galvanism, and chemical affinity. Superinduce magnetism at one end of a needle, the opposite magnetism takes place at the other end. If the south attracts, the north repels. To empty here, you must condense there. An inevitable dualism bisects nature, so that each thing is a half, and suggests another thing to make it whole; as, spirit, matter; man, woman; odd, even; subjective, objective; in, out; upper, under; motion, rest; yea, nay.

Whilst the world is thus dual, so is every one of its parts. The entire system of things gets represented in every particle. There is somewhat that resembles the ebb and flow of the sea, day and night, man and woman, in a single needle of the pine, in a kernel of corn, in each individual of every animal tribe. The reaction, so grand in the elements, is repeated within these small boundaries. For example, in the animal kingdom the physiologist has observed that no creatures are favorites, but a certain compensation balances every gift and every defect. A surplusage given to one part is paid out of a reduction from another part of the same creature. If the head and neck are enlarged, the trunk and extremities are cut short.

The theory of the mechanic forces is another example. What we gain in power is lost in time, and the converse. The periodic or compensating errors of the planets is another instance. The influences of climate and soil in political history are another. The cold climate invigorates. The barren soil does not breed fevers, crocodiles, tigers, or scorpions.

The same dualism underlies the nature and condition of mankind. Every excess causes a defect; every defect an excess. Every sweet hath its sour; every evil its good. Every faculty which is a receiver of pleasure has an equal penalty put on its abuse. It is to answer for its moderation with its life. For every grain of wit there is a grain of folly. For every thing you have missed, you have gained something else; and for every thing you gain, you lose something. If riches increase, they are increased that use them. If the gatherer gathers too much, Nature takes out of us what it put into our chest; swells the estate, but kills the owner. Nature hates monopolies and exceptions. The waves of the sea do not more speedily seek a level from their loftiest tossing than the varieties of condition tend to equalize themselves. There is always some levelling circumstance that puts down the overbearing, the strong, the rich, the fortunate, substantially on the same ground with all others. Is an individual too strong and fierce for society and by temper and position a bad citizen—a morose ruffian, with a dash of the pirate spirit?—Nature sends them a troop of pretty sons and daughters who are getting along in the dame's classes at the village school, and love and fear for them smooths their grim scowl to courtesy. Thus Nature contrives to intenerate the granite and felspar, takes the boar out and puts the lamb in and keeps its balance true.

The farmer imagines power and place are fine things. But the President has paid dear for his White House. It has commonly cost him all his peace, and the best of his manly attributes. To preserve for a short time so conspicuous an appearance before the world, he is content to eat dust before the real masters who stand erect behind the throne. Or, are there those who desire the more substantial and permanent grandeur of genius?

Neither has this an immunity. The one who by force of will or of thought is great and overlooks thousands, has the charges of that eminence. With every influx of light comes new danger. Have they light? They must bear witness to the light, and always outrun that sympathy which gives them such keen satisfaction, by their fidelity to new revelations of the incessant soul. They must hate father and mother, wife and child. Has he all that the world loves and admires and covets?—they must cast behind themselves their admiration, and afflict themselves by faithfulness to their truth, and become a byword and a hissing.

This law writes the laws of cities and nations. It is in vain to build or plot or combine against it. Things refuse to be mismanaged long. *Res nolunt diu male administrari.* Though no checks to a new evil appear, the checks exist, and will appear. If the government is cruel, the governor's life is not safe. If you tax too high, the revenue will yield nothing. If you make the criminal code sanguinary, juries will not convict. If the law is too mild, private vengeance comes in. If the government is a terrific democracy, the pressure is resisted by an over-charge of energy in the citizen, and life glows with a fiercer flame. The true life and satisfaction of all seem to elude the utmost rigors or felicities of condition and to establish themselves with great indifference under all varieties of circumstances. Under all governments the influence of character remains the same—in Turkey and in New England about alike. Under the primeval despots of Egypt, history honestly confesses that individuals must have been as free as culture could make them.

These appearances indicate the fact that the universe is represented in every one of its particles. Every thing in nature contains all the powers of nature. Every thing is made of one hidden stuff; as the naturalist sees one type under every metamorphosis, and regards a horse as a running man, a fish as a swimming man, a bird as a flying man, a tree as a rooted man. Each new form repeats not only the main character of the type, but part for part all the details, all the aims, furtherances, hindrances, energies, and whole system of every other. Every occupation, trade, art, transaction, is a compend of the world and a correlative of every other. Each one is an entire emblem of human life; of its good and ill, its trials, its enemies, its course, and its end. And each one must somehow accommodate the whole person and recite all their destiny.

The world globes itself in a drop of dew. The microscope cannot find the animalcule which is less perfect for being little. Eyes, ears, taste, smell, motion, resistance, appetite, and organs of reproduction that take hold on eternity—all find room to consist in the small

creature. So do we put our life into every act. The true
doctrine of omnipresence is that God reappears in total
completeness in every moss and cobweb. The value of
the universe contrives to throw itself into every point.
If the good is there, so is the evil; if the affinity, so the
repulsion; if the force, so the limitation.

Thus is the universe alive. All things are moral. That
soul which within us is a sentiment, outside of us is a law.
We feel its inspiration; out there in history we can see its
fatal strength. "It is in the world, and the world was made
by it." Justice is not postponed. A perfect equity adjusts
its balance in all parts of life. Ἀεὶ γὰρ εὖ πίπτουσιν οἱ
Διὸς κύβοι—The dice of God are always loaded. The
world looks like a multiplication-table, or a mathematical equation, which, turn it how you will, balances itself.
Take what figure you will, its exact value, nor more nor
less, still returns to you. Every secret is told, every crime is
punished, every virtue rewarded, every wrong redressed,
in silence and certainty. What we call retribution is the
universal necessity by which the whole appears wherever
a part appears. If you see smoke, there must be fire. If
you see a hand or a limb, you know that the trunk to
which it belongs is there behind.

Every act rewards itself, or, in other words integrates
itself, in a twofold manner; first in the thing, or in real
nature; and secondly in the circumstance, or in appar-

ent nature. People call the circumstance the retribution. The causal retribution is in the thing and is seen by the soul. The retribution in the circumstance is seen by the understanding; it is inseparable from the thing, but is often spread over a long time and so does not become distinct until after many years. The specific stripes may follow late after the offence, but they follow because they accompany it. Crime and punishment grow out of one stem. Punishment is a fruit that unsuspectedly ripens within the flower of the pleasure which concealed it. Cause and effect, means and ends, seed and fruit, cannot be severed; for the effect already blooms in the cause, the end preexists in the means, the fruit in the seed.

Whilst thus the world will be whole and refuses to be disparted, we seek to act partially, to sunder, to appropriate; for example, to gratify the senses we sever the pleasure of the senses from the needs of the character. The ingenuity of human nature has always been dedicated to the solution of one problem—how to detach the sensual sweet, the sensual strong, the sensual bright, etc., from the moral sweet, the moral deep, the moral fair; that is, again, to contrive to cut clean off this upper surface so thin as to leave it bottomless; to get a *one end*, without an *other end*. The soul says, "Eat"; the body would feast. The soul says, "The man and woman shall be one flesh and one soul"; the body would join the flesh only. The soul says, "Have dominion over all things to the ends of virtue"; the body would have the power over things to its own ends.

The soul strives amain to live and work through all things. It would be the only fact. All things shall be added unto it—power, pleasure, knowledge, beauty. The particular type aim to be somebody; to set up for themselves; to truck and higgle for a private good; and, in particulars, to ride that they may ride; to dress that they may be dressed; to eat that they may eat; and to govern, that they may be seen. For those that seek to be great; they would have offices, wealth, power, and fame. They think that to be great is to possess one side of nature—the sweet, without the other side, the bitter.

Steadily is this dividing and detaching counteracted. Up to this day it must be owned no projector has had the smallest success. The parted water reunites behind our hand. Pleasure is taken out of pleasant things, profit out of profitable things, power out of strong things, as soon as we seek to separate them from the whole. We can no more halve things and get the sensual good, by itself, than we can get an inside that shall have no out-side, or a light without a shadow. "Drive out Nature with a fork, it comes running back."

Life invests itself with inevitable conditions, which the unwise seek to dodge, which one and another brags that they do not know, that they do not touch them—but the brag is on their own lips, the conditions are in their own soul. If they escape them in one part they attack them in another more vital part. If they have escaped them in form and in the appearance, it is because they have resisted their life and fled from themselves, and the retribution is so much death. So signal is the failure of all attempts to make this separation of the good from the tax, that the experiment would not be tried—since to try it is to be mad—but for the circumstance, that when the disease began in the will, of rebellion and separation, the intellect is at once infected, so that they cease to see God whole in each object, but are able to see the sensual allurement of an object and not see the sensual hurt; they see the mermaid's head but not the dragon's tail, and think they can cut off that which they would have from that which they would not have. "How secret art thou who dwellest in the highest heavens in silence, O thou only great God, sprinkling with an unwearied providence certain penal blindnesses upon such as have unbridled desires!"[1]

The human soul is true to these facts in the painting of fable, of history, of law, of proverbs, of conversation. It finds a tongue in literature unawares. Thus the Greeks called Jupiter, Supreme Mind; but having

[1] St. Augustine, Confessions, B. I.

traditionally ascribed to him many base actions, they involuntarily made amends to reason by tying up the hands of so bad a god. He is made as helpless as a king of England. Prometheus knows one secret which Jove must bargain for; Minerva, another. He cannot get his own thunders; Minerva keeps the key of them: "Of all the gods, I only know the keys that open the solid doors within whose vaults His thunders sleep."

A plain confession of the in-working of the All and of its moral aim. The Indian mythology ends in the same ethics; and it would seem impossible for any fable to be invented and get any currency which was not moral. Aurora forgot to ask youth for her lover, and though Tithonus is immortal, he is old. Achilles is not quite invulnerable; the sacred waters did not wash the heel by which Thetis held him. Siegfried, in the Nibelungen, is not quite immortal, for a leaf fell on his back whilst he was bathing in the dragon's blood, and that spot which it covered is mortal. And so it must be. There is a crack in every thing God has made. It would seem there is always this vindictive circumstance stealing in at unawares even into the wild poesy in which the human fancy attempted to make bold holiday and to shake itself free of the old laws—this back-stroke, this kick of the gun, certifying that the law is fatal; that in nature nothing can be given, all things are sold.

This is that ancient doctrine of Nemesis, who keeps watch in the universe and lets no offence go unchastised. The Furies they said are attendants on justice, and if the sun in heaven should transgress his path they would punish him. The poets related that stone walls and iron swords and leathern thongs had an occult sympathy with the wrongs of their owners; that the belt which Ajax gave Hector dragged the Trojan hero over the field at the wheels of the car of Achilles, and the sword which Hector gave Ajax was that on whose point Ajax fell. They recorded that when the Thasians erected a statue to Theagenes, a victor in the games, one of his rivals went to it by night and endeavored to throw it down by repeated blows, until at last he moved it from its pedestal and was crushed to death beneath its fall.

This voice of fable has in it somewhat divine. It came from thought above the will of the writer. That is the best part of each writer which has nothing private in it; that which a writer does not know; that which flowed out of their constitution and not from their too active invention; that which in the study of a single artist you might not easily find, but in the study of many you would abstract as the spirit of them all. Phidias it is not, but the work of some other in that early Hellenic world, that I would know. The name and circumstance of Phidias, however convenient for history, embarrass when we come to the highest criticism. We are to see that which someone was tending to do in a given period, and was hindered, or, if you will, modified in doing, by the interfering volitions of Phidias, of Dante, of Shakespeare, the organ whereby another at the moment wrought.

Still more striking is the expression of this fact in the proverbs of all nations, which are always the literature of reason, or the statements of an absolute truth without qualification. Proverbs, like the sacred books of each nation, are the sanctuary of the intuitions. That which the droning world, chained to appearances, will not allow the realist to say in their own words, it will suffer them to say in proverbs without contradiction. And this law of laws, which the pulpit, the senate and the college deny, is hourly preached in all markets and workshops by flights of proverbs, whose teaching is as true and as omnipresent as that of birds and flies.

All things are double, one against another.—Tit for tat; an eye for an eye; a tooth for a tooth; blood for blood; measure for measure; love for love.—Give and it shall be given you.—The one that watereth shall be watered as well.—What will you have? quoth God; pay for it and take it.—Nothing venture, nothing have.— Thou shalt be paid exactly for what thou hast done, no more, no less.—Who doth not work shall not eat.—

Harm watch, harm catch.—Curses always recoil on the head of the one who imprecates them.—If you put a chain around the neck of a slave, the other end fastens itself around your own.—Bad counsel confounds the adviser.—The Devil is an ass.

It is thus written, because it is thus in life. Our action is overmastered and characterized above our will by the law of nature. We aim at a petty end quite aside from the public good, but our act arranges itself by irresistible magnetism in a line with the poles of the world.

One cannot speak but be judged themselves. With one's will or against one's will they draw their portrait to the eye of their companions by every word. Every opinion reacts on the one who utters it. It is a thread-ball thrown at a mark, but the other end remains in the thrower's bag. Or rather it is a harpoon hurled at the whale, unwinding, as it flies, a coil of cord in the boat, and, if the harpoon is not good, or not well thrown, it will go nigh to cut the steersman in twain or to sink the boat.

You cannot do wrong without suffering wrong. "No man had ever a point of pride that was not injurious to him," said Burke. The exclusive in fashionable life does not see that they exclude themselves from enjoyment, in the attempt to appropriate it. The exclusionist in religion does not see that they shut the door of heaven on themselves, in striving to shut out others. Treat others as pawns and ninepins and you shall suffer as well as they. If you leave out their heart, you shall lose your own. The senses would make things of all persons; of women, of children, of the poor. The vulgar proverb, "I will get it from his purse or get it from his skin," is sound philosophy.

All infractions of love and equity in our social relations are speedily punished. They are punished by fear. Whilst I stand in simple relations to my peers, I have no displeasure in meeting them. We meet as water meets water, or as two currents of air mix, with perfect diffusion and interpenetration of nature. But as soon as there is any departure from simplicity, and attempt at halfness, or good for me that is not good for them, my neighbor feels the wrong; they shrink from me as far as I have shrunk from them; their eyes no longer seek mine; there is war between us; there is hate in them and fear in me.

All the old abuses in society, universal and particular, all unjust accumulations of property and power, are avenged in the same manner. Fear is an instructor of great sagacity and the herald of all revolutions. One thing fear teaches, that there is rottenness where it appears. Fear is a carrion crow, and though you see not well what it hovers for, there is death somewhere. Our property is timid, our laws are timid, our cultivated classes are timid. Fear for ages has boded and mowed and gibbered over government and property. That obscene bird is not there for nothing. He indicates great wrongs which must be revised.

Of the like nature is that expectation of change which instantly follows the suspension of our voluntary activity. The terror of cloudless noon, the emerald of Polycrates, the awe of prosperity, the instinct which leads every generous soul to impose on itself tasks of a noble asceticism and vicarious virtue, are the tremblings of the balance of justice through the heart and mind of humanity.

Experienced people of the world know very well that it is best to pay scot and lot as they go along, and that one often pays dear for a small frugality. The borrower runs in their own debt. Has one gained anything who has received a hundred favors and rendered none? Has one gained by borrowing, through indolence or cunning, their neighbor's wares, or horses, or money? There arises on the deed the instant acknowledgment of benefit on the one part and of debt on the other; that is, of superiority and inferiority. The transaction remains in the memory of themselves and their neighbor; and every new transaction alters according to its nature their relation to each other. One may soon come to see that he had better have broken their own bones than to have ridden in their neighbor's coach, and that "the highest price one can pay for a thing is to ask for it."

The wise will extend this lesson to all parts of life, and know that it is the part of prudence to face every claimant and pay every just demand on your time, your talents, or your heart. Always pay; for first or last you must pay your entire debt. Persons and events may stand for a time between you and justice, but it is only a postponement. You must pay at last your own debt. If you are wise you will dread a prosperity which only loads you with more. Benefit is the end of nature. But for every benefit which you receive, a tax is levied. The great are those who confer the most benefits. To receive favors and render none, those are the one base thing in the universe. In the order of nature we cannot render benefits to those from whom we receive them, or only seldom. But the benefit we receive must be rendered again, line for line, deed for deed, cent for cent, to somebody. Beware of too much good staying in your hand. It will fast corrupt and worm worms. Pay it away quickly in some sort.

Labor is watched over by the same pitiless laws. Cheapest, say the prudent, is the dearest labor. What we buy in a broom, a mat, a wagon, a knife, is some application of good sense to a common want. It is best to pay in your land a skillful gardener, or to buy good sense applied to gardening; in your sailor, good sense applied to navigation; in the house, good sense applied to cooking, sewing, serving; in your agent, good sense applied to accounts and affairs. So do you multiply your presence, or spread yourself throughout your estate. But because of the dual constitution of things, in labor as in life there can be no cheating. The thieves steal from themselves. The swindlers swindle themselves. For the real price of labor is knowledge and virtue, whereof wealth and credit are signs. These signs, like paper money, may be counterfeited or stolen, but that which they represent, namely, knowledge and virtue, cannot be counterfeited or stolen. These ends of labor cannot be answered but by real exertions of the mind, and in obedience to pure motives. The cheat, the defaulter, the gambler, cannot extort the knowledge of material and moral nature which his honest care and pains yield to the operative. The law of nature is, Do the thing, and you shall have the Power; but they who do not the thing have not the power.

Human labor, through all its forms, from the sharpening of a stake to the construction of a city or an epic, is one immense illustration of the perfect compensation of the universe. The absolute balance of Give and Take, the doctrine that everything has its price—and if that price is not paid, not that thing but something else is obtained, and that it is impossible to get anything without its price—is not less sublime in the columns of a ledger than in the budgets of states, in the laws of light and darkness, in all the action and reaction of nature. I cannot doubt that the high laws which all see implicated in those processes with which they are conversant, the stern ethics which sparkle on his chisel-edge, which are measured out by his plumb and foot-rule, which stand as manifest in the footing of the shop-bill as in the history of a state—do recommend to them their trade, and though seldom named, exalt that business to their imagination.

The league between virtue and nature engages all things to assume a hostile front to vice. The beautiful laws and substances of the world persecute and whip the traitor. He finds that things are arranged for truth and benefit, but there is no den in the wide world to hide a rogue. Commit a crime, and the earth is made of glass. Commit a crime, and it seems as if a coat of snow fell on the ground, such as reveals in the woods the track of every partridge and fox and squirrel and mole. You cannot recall the spoken word, you cannot wipe out the foot-track, you cannot draw up the ladder, so as to leave no inlet or clew. Some damning circumstance always transpires. The laws and substances of nature—water, snow, wind, gravitation—become penalties to the thief.

On the other hand the law holds with equal sureness

for all right action. Love, and you shall be loved. All love is mathematically just, as much as the two sides of an algebraic equation. The good souls have absolute good, which like fire turns everything to its own nature, so that you cannot do them any harm; but as the royal armies sent against Napoleon, when he approached cast down their colors and from enemies became friends, so disasters of all kinds, as sickness, offence, poverty, prove benefactors:

"Winds blow and waters roll

Strength to the brave,

and power and deity,

Yet in themselves are nothing."

The good are befriended even by weakness and defect. As no one had ever a point of pride that was not injurious to them, so no one had ever a defect that was not somewhere made useful to them. The stag in the fable admired his horns and blamed his feet, but when the hunter came, his feet saved him, and afterwards, caught in the thicket, his horns destroyed him. All people in their lifetime need to thank their faults. As no one thoroughly understands a truth until they have contended against it, so no one has a thorough acquaintance with the hindrances or talents of others until they have suffered from one and seen the triumph of the other over their own want of the same. Have they a defect of temper that unfits them to live in society? Thereby they are driven to entertain themselves alone and acquire habits of self-help; and thus, like the wounded oyster, they mend their shell with pearl.

Our strength grows out of our weakness. The indignation which arms itself with secret forces does not awaken until we are pricked and stung and sorely assailed. It is the great one who is willing to be little. Whilst they sit on the cushion of advantages, they go to sleep. When they are pushed, tormented, defeated, they have a chance to learn something; they have been put on their wits, on their fortitude; they have gained facts; learned their ignorance; are cured of the insanity of conceit; possess moderation and real skill. The wise ones throw themselves on the side of their assailants. It is more their own interest than it is theirs to find their own weak point. The wound cicatrizes and falls off from them like a dead skin and when they would triumph, lo! they have passed on invulnerable. Blame is safer than praise. I hate to be defended in a newspaper. As long as all that is said is said against me, I feel a certain assurance of success. But as soon as honeyed words of praise are spoken for me I feel as one that lies unprotected before his enemies. In general, every evil to which we do not succumb is a benefactor. As the Sandwich Islanders believe that the strength and valor of the enemy they kill passes into themselves, so we gain the strength of the temptation we resist.

The same guards which protect us from disaster, defect, and enmity, defend us, if we will, from selfishness and fraud. Bolts and bars are not the best of our institutions, nor is shrewdness in trade a mark of wisdom. People suffer all their life long under the foolish superstition that they can be cheated. But it is as impossible for someone to be cheated by anyone but themselves, as for a thing to be and not to be at the same time. There is a third silent party to all our bargains. The nature and soul of things takes on itself the guaranty of the fulfilment of every contract, so that honest service cannot come to loss. If you serve an ungrateful master, serve them the more. Put God in your debt. Every stroke shall be repaid. The longer the payment is withholden, the better for you; for compound interest on compound interest is the rate and usage of this exchequer.

The history of persecution is a history of endeavors to cheat nature, to make water run up hill, to twist a rope of sand. It makes no difference whether the actors be many or one, a tyrant or a mob. A mob is a society of bodies voluntarily bereaving themselves of reason and traversing its work. The mob is society voluntarily descending to the nature of the beast. Its fit hour of activity is night. Its actions are insane like its whole constitution. It persecutes a principle; it would whip a right; it would tar and feather justice, by inflicting fire and outrage upon the houses and persons of those who have these. It resembles the pranks of boys, who run with fire-engines to put out the ruddy aurora streaming to the stars. The inviolate spirit turns their spite against the wrongdoers. The martyr cannot be dishonored. Every lash inflicted is a tongue of fame; every prison, a more illustrious abode; every burned book or house enlightens the world; every suppressed or expunged word reverberates through the earth from side to side. Hours of sanity and consideration are always arriving to communities, as to individuals, when the truth is seen and the martyrs are justified.

Thus do all things preach the indifferency of circumstances. The human spirit is all. Every thing has two sides, a good and an evil. Every advantage has its tax. I learn to be content. But the doctrine of compensation is not the doctrine of indifferency. The thoughtless say, on hearing these representations—What boots it to do well? There is one event to good and evil; if I gain any good I must pay for it; if I lose any good I gain some other; all actions are indifferent.

There is a deeper fact in the soul than compensation, to wit, its own nature. The soul is not a compensation, but a life. The soul is. Under all this running sea of circumstance, whose waters ebb and flow with perfect balance, lies the aboriginal abyss of real Being. Essence, or God, is not a relation or a part, but the whole. Being is the vast affirmative, excluding negation, self-balanced, and swallowing up all relations, parts, and times within itself. Nature, truth, virtue are the influx from thence. Vice is the absence or departure of the same. Nothing, Falsehood, may indeed stand as the great Night or shade on which as a background the living universe paints itself forth, but no fact is begotten by it; it cannot work, for it is not. It cannot work any good; it cannot work any harm. It is harm inasmuch as it is worse not to be than to be.

We feel defrauded of the retribution due to evil acts, because the criminal adheres to his vice and contumacy and does not come to a crisis or judgment anywhere in visible nature. There is no stunning confutation of his nonsense before others and angels. Has he therefore outwitted the law? Inasmuch as he carries the malignity and the lie with him he so far deceases from nature. In some manner there will be a demonstration of the wrong to the understanding also; but, should we not see it, this deadly deduction makes square the eternal account.

Neither can it be said, on the other hand, that the gain of rectitude must be bought by any loss. There is no penalty to virtue; no penalty to wisdom; they are proper additions of being. In a virtuous action I properly *am*; in a virtuous act I add to the world; I plant into deserts conquered from Chaos and Nothing and see the darkness receding on the limits of the horizon. There can be no excess to love, none to knowledge, none to beauty, when these attributes are considered in the purest sense. The soul refuses limits, and always affirms an Optimism, never a Pessimism.

One's life is a progress, and not a station. One's instinct is trust. Our instinct uses "more" and "less" in application to others, of the *presence of the soul*, and not of its absence, the brave soul is greater than the coward; the true, the benevolent, the wise, is more upstanding and not less, than the fool and knave. There is no tax on the good of virtue, for that is the incoming of God wholly, or absolute existence, without any comparative. Material good has its tax, and if it came without desert or sweat, has no root in me, and the next wind will blow it away. But all the good of nature is the soul's, and may be had if paid for in nature's lawful coin, that is, by labor which the heart and the head allow. I no longer wish to meet a good I do not earn, for example to find a pot of buried gold, knowing that it brings with it new burdens. I do not wish more external goods— neither possessions, nor honors, nor powers, nor persons. The gain is apparent; the tax is certain. But there is no tax on the knowledge that the compensation exists and that it is not desirable to dig up treasure. Herein I rejoice with a serene eternal peace. I contract the boundaries of possible mischief. I learn the wisdom of St. Bernard—"Nothing can work me damage except myself; the harm that I sustain I carry about with me, and never am a real sufferer but by my own fault."

In the nature of the soul is the compensation for the inequalities of condition. The radical tragedy of nature seems to be the distinction of More and Less. How can Less not feel the pain; how not feel indignation or malevolence towards More? Look at those who have less faculty, and one feels sad and knows not well what to make of it. They almost shun their eyes; they fear they will upbraid God. What should they do? It seems a great injustice. But see the facts nearly and these mountainous inequalities vanish. Love reduces them as the sun melts the iceberg in the sea. The heart and soul of all humanity being one, this bitterness of *Theirs and Mine* ceases. Theirs is mine. I am my brother and my brother is me. If I feel overshadowed and outdone by great neighbors, I can yet love; I can still receive; and they that loveth maketh their own the grandeur they love. Thereby I make the discovery that my brother is my guardian, acting for me with the friendliest designs, and the estate I so admired and envied is my own. It is the nature of the soul to appropriate all things. Jesus and Shakespeare are fragments of the soul, and by love I conquer and incorporate them in my own conscious domain. God's virtue—is not that mine? God's wit—if it cannot be made mine, it is not wit.

Such also is the natural history of calamity. The changes which break up at short intervals the prosperity of some are advertisements of a nature whose law is growth. Every soul is by this intrinsic necessity quitting its whole system of things, its friends and home and laws and faith, as the shell-fish crawls out of its beautiful but stony case, because it no longer admits of its growth, and slowly forms a new house. In proportion to the vigor of the individual these revolutions are frequent, until in some happier mind they are incessant and all worldly relations hang very loosely from them, becoming as it were a transparent fluid membrane through which the living form is seen, and not, as in most others, an indurated heterogeneous fabric of many dates and of no settled character, in which the individual is imprisoned. Then there can be enlargement, and people of to-day scarcely recognize themselves of yesterday. And such should be the outward biography of people in time, a putting off of dead circumstances day by day, as they renew their raiment day by day. But to us, in our lapsed estate, resting, not advancing, resisting, not cooperating with the divine expansion, this growth comes by shocks.

We cannot part with our friends. We cannot let our angels go. We do not see that they only go out that arch-angels may come in. We are idolaters of the old. We do not believe in the riches of the soul, in its proper eternity and omnipresence. We do not believe there is any force in today to rival or re-create that beautiful yesterday. We linger in the ruins of the old tent where once we had bread and shelter and organs, nor believe that the spirit can feed, cover, and nerve us again. We cannot again find aught so dear, so sweet, so graceful. But we sit and weep in vain. The voice of the Almighty saith, "Up and onward for evermore!" We cannot stay amid the ruins. Neither will we rely on the new; and so we walk ever with reverted eyes, like those monsters who look backwards.

And yet the compensations of calamity are made apparent to the understanding also, after long intervals of time. A fever, a mutilation, a cruel disappointment, a loss of wealth, a loss of friends, seem at the moment unpaid loss, and unpayable. But the sure years reveal the deep remedial force that underlies all facts. The death of a dear friend, wife, brother, lover, which seemed nothing but privation, somewhat later assumes the aspect of a guide or genius; for it commonly operates revolutions in our way of life, terminates an epoch of infancy or of youth which was waiting to be closed, breaks up a wonted occupation, or a household, or style of living, and allows the formation of new ones more friendly to the growth of character. It permits or constrains the formation of new acquaintances and the reception of new influences that prove of the first importance to the next years; and the man or woman who would have remained a sunny garden-flower, with no room for its roots and too much sunshine for its head, by the falling of the walls and the neglect of the gardener is made the banian of the forest, yielding shade and fruit to wide neighborhoods of others.

QUESTIONS TO CONSIDER:

1. What was the worst thing that ever happened to you?

2. Can you link that event (see #1) to a greater good later on in your life?

3. If this is a holographic universe, what does that say about you personally?

4. What goes around comes around. Give examples of this from your own experience.

5. How could you be more of a participant in the circulation of energy that promotes life?

6. What is your current Self-Identity?

7. Explain Emerson's remark, "You will never see anything worse than yourselves."

8. "The affect of every action is measured by the depth of the sentiment from which it proceeds." What does this say to you about intention, passion and conviction?

9. Relate #8 with Holmes' teaching on the Law of Mind and manifestation.

10. "Be and not seem" is a famous quote of Emerson. How does it relate to you in today's world?

Circles
Emerson the Synthesizer

Overview:

CIRCULAR PATTERNS ARE PERVASIVE
THROUGHOUT THE NATURAL WORLD. A CIRCLE
IS "THE HIGHEST EMBLEM IN THE CIPHER OF
THE WORLD," WRITES EMERSON. THE UNIVERSE
IS MADE UP OF CIRCLES, REPEATED WITHOUT
END. TO HELP THE STUDENT OF SPIRITUALITY
UNDERSTAND THEIR OWN PART IN THE GREAT
SPHERICAL DANCE, EMERSON EXPLORES IN THIS
ESSAY THE LIFE-AFFIRMING POWER THAT
CIRCLES HAVE IN OUR LIVES.

EMERSON BEGINS BY QUOTING St. Augustine: "The nature of God is best described as a circle whose center is everywhere and its circumference nowhere." He harkens back to the essay on Compensation: "Consider the circular or compensatory character of every human action." Here we are again with the concept of return on investment; cause and effect inherent in each other. Ernest Holmes would agree. Holmes taught that the cause was in the effect and the effect was in the cause. This is one of the basic laws of life. The seed is in the apple, the apple is in the seed and so on. Holmes taught that by looking at a situation as an effect of a particular cause, we can create a new effect by initiating a new cause.

The image of a circle being how life moves, pressing outward, widening the circle, is markedly different from our linear image of time flowing in a straight line. They are two opposite perceptions of Reality. Linear thinking suggests an end, a stoppage. The circle is ever expanding, including more and more diversity. There are, Emerson wrote, "no fixtures in nature." Every end is a beginning. The universe is fluid and volatile. Permanence is but a word of degrees. When we see that all facts are fluid, we begin to see how much influence we have over our immediate experience. He wrote that the law dissolves the fact and holds it fluid. There is a lovely Gershwin song that states the case well: "In time the Rockies may tumble, Gibraltar will crumble, they're only made of clay, but our Love is here to stay." Yes Love (God) is ever present through the changing times, untroubled by the shifting sands.

One can hear the Buddhist influence in Emerson's writings, which helped to lay the groundwork for

Holmes. Within Holmes' writings, one can find this influence when he says to the effect that the fluidity of facts gives us enormous power over them. Nothing can stay the same without the influx of an agreeing consciousness. Quantum physics asserts that nothing in the objective world can exist without an apprehending mind. Indeed, that mind shapes the potential into a personal experience of it. In other words, when we change our belief by whatever means, the facts must reflect the new idea. Emerson notes how much more powerful the hand that built the granite wall is over the wall (effect) itself. This is what Holmes would later echo in: "We are always greater than the experience we are having or have had."

In "Circles," Emerson sees through appearances into the patterns within them. He sees the entire universe as a moving circle, in a sense. It is more than "What goes around comes around." He is speaking of a unified field, an unbroken connection between all the disparate parts of existence. He states, as Holmes does, that behind the coarse effect is a finer cause. That Cause is our potential, untapped and forever available. There is an emphasis on the temporariness of all material form. "New arts destroy the old."

Emerson sees an evolutionary principle in humanity. Holmes taught that when we become aware of this, we then must consciously direct evolution. "Life is a self-evolving circle, which, from a ring imperceptibly small rushes on all sides outwards to new and larger circles." Holmes would classify this as the natural tendency of "God" to make ever more of itself, never repeating, always rising above previous incarnations. Meister Eckhart said: "God is forever begetting the only Begotten." Holmes taught: "God makes everything out of itself by becoming the thing it makes." I always add, "and so do we." We raise the quality of our life by raising the content of our Mind, which acts as direction to the connective consciousness, drawing to itself what belongs with it.

"Life is a series of surprises," Emerson declared. He acknowledges that we can somewhat predict outcomes when we are engaged in routine, but "the masterpieces of God," which involve the growth of our soul, the leaps of awareness, are incalculable. When we allow the soul (essential Self) to be led, guided, and directed by the higher power of Spirit, the most surprising and delightful results can come through us. He is building the case for that trust we must have in the responsiveness of the universe. Locally we may call it the Law of Attraction, but it is more like a Law of Vibration. We draw from within the circle we inhabit. If we inhabit the circle (vibration) of love, we will find love everywhere. This Law applies also to Vitality, Abundance, Peace, and Joy. If we live in the expectation of Creative ideas, we will never run out of them.

At the close of the essay Emerson wrote: "The one thing we seek with insatiable desire is to forget ourselves, to be surprised out of propriety, to lose our sempiternal memory, to do something without knowing how or why; in short, to draw a new circle."

—Dr. Carol Carnes

Circles

Ralph Waldo Emerson

THE EYE IS THE FIRST CIRCLE; the horizon which it forms is the second; and throughout nature this primary figure is repeated without end. It is the highest emblem in the cipher of the world. St. Augustine described the nature of God as a circle whose center was everywhere and its circumference nowhere. We are all our lifetime reading the copious sense of this first of forms. One moral we have already deduced, in considering the circular or compensatory character of every human action. Another analogy we shall now trace, that every action admits of being outdone. Our life is an apprenticeship to the truth that around every circle another can be drawn; that there is no end in nature, but every end is a beginning; that there is always another dawn risen on mid-noon, and under every deep a lower deep opens.

This fact, as far as it symbolizes the moral fact of the Unattainable, the flying Perfect, around which the hands of one can never meet, at once the inspirer and the condemner of every success, may conveniently serve us to connect many illustrations of human power in every department.

There are no fixtures in nature. The universe is fluid and volatile. Permanence is but a word of degrees. Our globe seen by God is a transparent law, not a mass of facts. The law dissolves the fact and holds it fluid. Our culture is the predominance of an idea which draws after it this train of cities and institutions. Let us rise into another idea: they will disappear. The Greek sculpture is all melted away, as if it had been statues of ice; here and there a solitary figure or fragment remaining, as we see flecks and scraps of snow left in cold dells and mountain clefts in June and July. For the genius that created it creates now somewhat else. The Greek letters last a little longer, but are already passing under the same sentence and tumbling into the inevitable pit which the creation of new thought opens for all that is old. The new continents are built out of the ruins of an old planet; the new races fed out of the decomposition of the foregoing. New arts destroy the old. See the investment of capital in aqueducts made useless by hydraulics; fortifications, by gunpowder; roads and canals, by railways; sails, by steam; steam by electricity.

You admire this tower of granite, weathering the hurts of so many ages. Yet a little waving hand built this huge wall, and that which builds is better than that which is built. The hand that built can topple it down much faster. Better than the hand and nimbler was the invisible thought which wrought through it; and thus ever, behind the coarse effect, is a fine cause, which, being narrowly seen, is itself the effect of a finer cause. Everything looks permanent until its secret is known. A rich estate appears to some a firm and lasting fact; to a merchant, one easily created out of any materials, and easily lost. An orchard, good tillage, good grounds, seem a fixture, like a gold mine, or a river, to a citizen; but to a large farmer, not much more fixed than the state of the crop. Nature looks provokingly stable and secular, but it has a cause like all the rest; and when once I comprehend that, will these fields stretch so immovably wide, these leaves hang so individually considerable? Permanence is a word of degrees. Every thing is medial. Moons are no more bounds to spiritual power than bat-balls.

The key to every individual is their thought. Sturdy and defying though they look, they have a helm which they obey, which is the idea after which all their facts are classified. They can only be reformed by showing them a new idea which commands their own. One's life is a self-evolving circle, which, from a ring imperceptibly small, rushes on all sides outwards to new and larger circles, and that without end. The extent to which this generation of circles, wheel without wheel, will go, depends on the force or truth of the individual soul. For it is the inert effort of each thought, having formed itself into a circular wave of circumstance—as for instance an empire, rules of an art, a local usage, a religious rite—to heap itself on that ridge and to solidify and hem in the life. But if the soul is quick and strong it bursts over that boundary on all sides and expands another orbit on the great deep, which also runs up into a high wave, with attempt again to stop and to bind. But the heart refuses to be imprisoned; in its first and narrowest pulses, it already tends outward with a vast force and to immense and innumerable expansions.

Every ultimate fact is only the first of a new series. Every general law only a particular fact of some more general law presently to disclose itself. There is no outside, no inclosing wall, no circumference to us. As one finishes their story—how good! how final! how it puts a new face on all things! They fill the sky. Lo! on the other side rises also another and draws a circle around the circle we had just pronounced the outline of the sphere. Then already is our first speaker not themselves, but only a first speaker. Their only redress is forthwith to draw a circle outside of their antagonist. And so people do by themselves. The result of today, which haunts the mind and cannot be escaped, will presently be abridged into a word, and the principle that seemed to explain nature will itself be included as one example of a bolder generalization. In the thought of tomorrow there is a power to upheave all thy creed, all the creeds, all the literatures of the nations, and marshal thee to a heaven which no epic dream has yet depicted. Every individual is not so much a hired hand in the world as they are a suggestion of that they should be. We walk as prophecies of the next age.

Step by step we scale this mysterious ladder: The steps are actions; the new prospect is power. Every several result is threatened and judged by that which follows. Everyone seems to be contradicted by the new; it is only limited by the new. The new statement is always hated by the old, and, to those dwelling in the old, comes like an abyss of skepticism. But the eye soon gets wonted to it, for the eye and it are effects of one cause; then its innocency and benefit appear, and presently, all its energy spent, it pales and dwindles before the revelation of the new hour.

Fear not the new generalization. Does the fact look crass and material, threatening to degrade thy theory of spirit? Resist it not; it goes to refine and raise thy theory of matter just as much.

There are no fixtures to us, if we appeal to consciousness. Every person supposes themselves not to be fully understood; and if there is any truth in them, if they rest at last on the divine soul, I see not how it can be otherwise. The last chamber, the last closet, they must feel was never opened; there is always a residuum unknown, unanalyzable. That is, every soul believes that they have a greater possibility.

Our moods do not believe in each other. Today I am full of thoughts and can write what I please. I see no reason why I should not have the same thought, the same power of expression, tomorrow. What I write, whilst I write it, seems the most natural thing in the world; but yesterday I saw a dreary vacuity in this direction in which now I see so much; and a month hence, I doubt not, I shall wonder who he was that wrote so many continuous pages. Alas for this infirm faith, this will not strenuous, this vast ebb of a vast flow! I am God in nature; I am a weed by the wall.

The continual effort to raise above oneself, to work a pitch above the last height, betrays itself in one's relations. We thirst for approbation, yet cannot forgive the approver. The sweet of nature is love; yet, if I have a friend I am tormented by my imperfections. The love of me accuses the other party. If someone were high enough to slight me, then could I love them, and rise by my affection to new heights. One's growth is seen in the successive choirs of their friends. For every friend whom they lose for truth, they gain a better. I thought as I walked in the woods and mused on my friends, why should I play with them this game of idolatry? I know and see too well, when not voluntarily blind, the speedy limits of persons called high and worthy. Rich, noble, and great they are by the liberality of our speech, but truth is sad. O blessed Spirit, whom I forsake for these, they are not thou! Every personal consideration that we allow costs us heavenly state. We sell the thrones of angels for a short and turbulent pleasure.

How often must we learn this lesson? Others cease to interest us when we find their limitations. The only sin is limitation. As soon as you once come up with their limitations, it is all over with them. Have they talents? have they enterprise? have they knowledge? It boots not. Infinitely alluring and attractive was someone to you yesterday, a great hope, a sea to swim in; now, you have found their shore, found it a pond, and you care not if you never see it again.

Each new step we take in thought reconciles twenty seemingly discordant facts, as expressions of one law. Aristotle and Plato are reckoned the respective heads of two schools. The wise will see that Aristotle platon-izes. By going one step further back in thought, discor-dant opinions are reconciled by being seen to be two extremes of one principle, and we can never go so far back as to preclude a still higher vision.

Beware when the great God lets loose a thinker on this planet. Then all things are at risk. It is as when a conflagration has broken out in a great city, and no one knows what is safe, or where it will end. There is not a piece of science but its flank may be turned tomorrow; there is not any literary reputation, not the so-called eternal names of fame, that may not be revised and condemned. The very hopes of humanity, the thoughts of its heart, the religion of nations, the manners and morals of mankind are all at the mercy of a new generalization. Generalization is always a new influx of the divinity into the mind. Hence the thrill that attends it.

Valor consists in the power of self-recovery, so that one cannot have their flank turned, cannot be out-generaled, but put them where you will, they stand. This can only be by their preferring truth to their past apprehension of truth, and their alert acceptance of it from whatever quarter; the intrepid conviction that their laws, their relations to society, their Christianity, their world, may at any time be superseded and decease.

There are degrees in idealism. We learn first to play with it academically, as the magnet was once a toy. Then we see in the heyday of youth and poetry that it may be true, that it is true in gleams and fragments. Then its countenance waxes stern and grand, and we see that it must be true. It now shows itself ethical and practical. We learn that God is; the Source in me; and that all things are shadows of God. The idealism of Berkeley is only a crude statement of the idealism of Jesus, and that again is a crude statement of the fact that all nature is the rapid efflux of goodness executing and organizing itself. Much more obviously is history and the state of the world at any one time directly dependent on the intellectual classification then existing in the minds of all. The things which are dear to people at this hour are so on account of the ideas which have emerged on their mental horizon, and which cause the present order of things, as a tree bears its apples. A new degree of culture would instantly revolutionize the entire system of human pursuits.

Conversation is a game of circles. In conversation we pluck up the *termini* which bound the common of silence on every side. The parties are not to be judged by the spirit they partake and even express under this Pentecost. Tomorrow they will have receded from this high-water mark. Tomorrow you shall find them stooping under the old pack-saddles. Yet let us enjoy the cloven flame whilst it glows on our walls. When each new speaker strikes a new light, emancipates us from the oppression of the last speaker, to oppress us with the greatness and exclusiveness of their own thought, then yields us to another redeemer, we seem to recover our rights, to become our own self. O, what truths profound and executable only in ages and orbs, are supposed in the announcement of every truth! In common hours, society sits cold and statuesque. We all stand waiting, empty—knowing, possibly, that we can be full, surrounded by mighty symbols which are not symbols to us, but prose and trivial toys. Then cometh the god and converts the statues into fiery men, and by a flash of their eye burns up the veil which shrouded all things, and the meaning of the very furniture, of cup and saucer, of chair and clock and tester, is manifest. The facts which loomed so large in the fogs of yesterday— property, climate, breeding, personal beauty, and the like have strangely changed their proportions. All that we reckoned settled shakes and rattles; and literatures, cities, climates, religions, leave their foundations and dance before our eyes. And yet here again see the swift circumspection! Good as is discourse, silence is better, and shames it. The length of the discourse indicates the distance of thought betwixt the speaker and the hearer. If they were at a perfect understanding in any part, no words would be necessary thereon. If at one in all parts, no words would be suffered.

Literature is a point outside of our hodiernal circle

through which a new one may be described. The use of literature is to afford us a platform whence we may command a view of our present life, a purchase by which we may move it. We fill ourselves with ancient learning, install ourselves the best we can in Greek, in Punic, in Roman houses, only that we may wiselier see French, English, and American houses and modes of living. In like manner we see literature best from the midst of wild nature, or from the din of affairs, or from a high religion. The field cannot be well seen from within the field. The astronomer must have the diameter of the earth's orbit as a base to find the parallax of any star.

Therefore we value the poet. All the argument and all the wisdom is not in the encyclopaedia, or the treatise on metaphysics, or the Body of Divinity, but in the sonnet or the play. In my daily work I incline to repeat my old steps, and do not believe in remedial force, in the power of change and reform. But some Petrarch or Ariosto, filled with the new wine of his imagination, writes me an ode or a brisk romance, full of daring thought and action. He smites and arouses me with his shrill tones, breaks up my whole chain of habits, and I open my eye on my own possibilities. He claps wings to the sides of all the solid old lumber of the world, and I am capable once more of choosing a straight path in theory and practice.

We have the same need to command a view of the religion of the world. We can never see Christianity from the catechism: from the pastures, from a boat in the pond, from amidst the songs of wood-birds we possibly may. Cleansed by the elemental light and wind, steeped in the sea of beautiful forms which the field offers us, we may chance to cast a right glance back upon biography. Christianity is rightly dear to the best of all; yet was there never a young philosopher whose breeding had fallen into the Christian church by whom that brave text of Paul's was not specially prized: "Then shall also the Son be subject unto Him who put all things under him, that God may be all in all." Let the claims and virtues of persons be never so great and welcome, the instinct within us all presses eagerly onward to the impersonal and illimitable, and gladly arms itself against the dogmatism of bigots with this generous word out of the book itself.

The natural world may be conceived of as a system of concentric circles, and we now and then detect in nature slight dislocations which apprise us that this surface on which we now stand is not fixed, but sliding. These manifold tenacious qualities, this chemistry and vegetation, these metals and animals, which seem to stand there for their own sake, are means and methods only—are words of God, and as fugitive as other words. Has the naturalist or chemist learned his craft, who has explored the gravity of atoms and the elective affinities, who has not yet discerned the deeper law whereof this is only a partial or approximate statement, namely that like draws to like, and that the goods which belong to you gravitate to you and need not be pursued with pains and cost? Yet is that statement approximate also, and not final. Omnipresence is a higher fact. Not through subtle subterranean channels need friend and fact be drawn to their counterpart, but, rightly considered, these things proceed from the eternal generation of the soul. Cause and effect are two sides of one fact.

The same law of eternal procession ranges all that we call the virtues, and extinguishes each in the light of a better. The great ones will not be prudent in the popular sense; all their prudence will be so much deduction from their grandeur. But it behooves each to see, when they sacrifice prudence, to what god they devote it; if to ease and pleasure, they had better be prudent still; if to a great trust, they can well spare their mule and panniers who has a winged chariot instead. Geoffrey draws on his boots to go through the woods, that his feet may be safer from the bite of snakes; Aaron never thinks of such a peril. In many years neither is harmed by such an accident. Yet it seems to me that with every precaution you take against such an evil you put yourself into the power of the evil. I suppose that the highest prudence is the lowest prudence. Is this too sudden a rushing from the center to the verge of our orbit? Think how many times we shall fall back into pitiful calculations before we take up our rest in the great sentiment, or make the verge of today the new center. Besides, your bravest sentiment is familiar to the humblest souls. The poor and the low have their way of expressing the last facts of philosophy as well as you. "Blessed be nothing" and "The worse things are, the better they are" are proverbs which express the transcendentalism of common life.

One's justice is another's injustice; one's beauty another's ugliness; one's wisdom another's folly; as one beholds the same objects from a higher point. Some think justice consists in paying debts, and has no measure in their abhorrence of another who is very remiss in this duty and makes the creditor wait tediously. But others have their own way of looking at things; asks themselves Which debt must I pay first, the debt to the rich, or the debt to the poor? the debt of money, or the debt of thought to mankind, of genius to nature? For you, O broker, there is no other principle but arithmetic. For me, commerce is of trivial import; love, faith, truth of character, the aspiration of humanity, these are sacred; nor can I detach one duty, like you, from all other duties, and concentrate my forces mechanically on the payment of moneys. Let me live onward; you shall find that, though slower, the progress of my character will liquidate all these debts without injustice to higher claims. If an individual should dedicate themselves to the payment of notes, would not this be injustice? Do they owe no debt but money? And are all claims on them to be postponed to a landlord's or a banker's?

There is no virtue which is final; all are initial. The virtues of society are vices of the saint. The terror of reform is the discovery that we must cast away our virtues, or what we have always esteemed such, into the same pit that has consumed our grosser vices: "Forgive thy crimes, forgive thy virtues too, Those smaller faults, half converts to the right."

It is the highest power of divine moments that they abolish our contritions also. I accuse myself of sloth and unprofitableness day by day; but when these waves of God flow into me I no longer reckon lost time. I no longer poorly compute my possible achievement by what remains to me of the month or the year; for these moments confer a sort of omnipresence and omnipotence which asks nothing of duration, but sees that the energy of the mind is commensurate with the work to be done, without time.

And thus, O circular philosopher, I hear some reader exclaim, you have arrived at a fine Pyrrhonism, at an equivalence and indifferency of all actions, and would fain teach us that *if we are true*, forsooth, our crimes may be lively stones out of which we shall construct the temple of the true God!

I am not careful to justify myself. I own I am gladdened by seeing the predominance of the saccharine principle throughout vegetable nature, and not less by beholding in morals that unrestrained inundation of the principle of good into every chink and hole that selfishness has left open, yea into selfishness and sin itself; so that no evil is pure, nor hell itself without its extreme satisfactions. But lest I should mislead any when I have my own head and obey my whims, let me remind the reader that I am only an experimenter. Do not set the least value on what I do, or the least discredit on what I do not, as if I pretended to settle any thing as true or false. I unsettle all things. No facts are to me sacred; none are profane; I simply experiment, an endless seeker with no Past at my back.

Yet this incessant movement and progression which all things partake could never become sensible to us but by contrast to some principle of fixture or stability in the soul. Whilst the eternal generation of circles proceeds, the eternal generator abides. That central life is somewhat superior to creation, superior to knowledge and thought, and contains all its circles. For ever it labors to create a life and thought as Large and excellent as itself, but in vain, for that which is made instructs how to make a better.

Thus there is no sleep, no pause, no preservation, but all things renew, germinate, and spring. Why should we import rags and relics into the new hour? Nature abhors the old, and old age seems the only disease; all others run into this one. We call it by many names—fever, intemperance, insanity, stupidity and crime; they are all forms of old age; they are rest, conservatism, appropriation, inertia; not newness, not the way onward. We grizzle every day. I see no need of it. Whilst we converse with what is above us, we do not grow old, but grow young. Infancy, youth, receptive, aspiring, with religious eye looking upward, counts itself nothing and abandons itself to the instruction flowing from all sides. But the man and woman of seventy assume to know all, they have outlived their hope, they renounce aspiration, accept the actual for the necessary, and talk down to the young. Let them, then, become organs of the Holy Ghost; let them be lovers; let them behold truth; and their eyes are uplifted, their wrinkles smoothed, they are perfumed again with hope and power. This old age ought not to creep on a human mind. In nature every moment is new; the past is always swallowed and forgotten; the coming only is sacred. Nothing is secure but life, transition, the energizing spirit. No love can be bound by oath or covenant to secure it against a higher love. No truth so sublime but it may be trivial tomorrow in the light of new thoughts. People wish to be settled; only as far as they are unsettled is there any hope for them.

Life is a series of surprises. We do not guess today the mood, the pleasure, the power of tomorrow, when we are building up our being. Of lower states, of acts of routine and sense, we can tell somewhat; but the masterpieces of God, the total growths and universal movements of the soul, he hideth; they are incalculable. I can know that truth is divine and helpful; but how it shall help me I can have no guess, for *so to be* is the sole inlet of *so to know*. The new position of the advancing society has all the powers of the old, yet has them all new. It carries in its bosom all the energies of the past, yet is itself an exhalation of the morning. I cast away in this new moment all my once hoarded knowledge, as vacant and vain. Now, for the first time seem I to know any thing rightly. The simplest words—we do not know what they mean except when we love and aspire.

The difference between talents and character is adroitness to keep the old and trodden round, and power and courage to make a new road to new and better goals. Character makes an overpowering present; a cheerful, determined hour, which fortifies all the company by making them see that much is possible and excellent that was not thought of. Character dulls the impression of particular events. When we see the conqueror we do not think much of any one battle or success. We see that we had exaggerated the difficulty. It was easy to him. The great victor is not convulsible or tormentable; events pass over him without much impression. People say sometimes, "See what I have overcome; see how cheerful I am; see how completely I have triumphed over these black events." Not if they still remind me of the black event. True conquest is the causing the calamity to fade and disappear as an early cloud of insignificant result in a history so large and advancing.

The one thing which we seek with insatiable desire is to forget ourselves, to be surprised out of our propriety, to lose our sempiternal memory and to do something without knowing how or why; in short to draw a new circle. Nothing great was ever achieved without enthusiasm. The way of life is wonderful; it is by abandonment. The great moments of history are the facilities of performance through the strength of ideas, as the works of genius and religion. "A man," said Oliver Cromwell, "never rises so high as when he knows not whither he is going." Dreams and drunkenness, the use of opium and alcohol are the semblance and counterfeit of this oracular genius, and hence their dangerous attraction. For the like reason they ask the aid of wild passions, as in gaming and war, to ape in some manner these flames and generosities of the heart.

QUESTIONS TO CONSIDER:

1. Describe the two perceptions of Reality: circular and linear.

2. What meaning does "all facts are fluid" hold for you?

3. Have you had the experience of an ending becoming a beginning?

4. What, if anything, do you consider permanent in Nature?

5. What does Emerson mean when he says, "Beware when the great God lets loose a thinker"?

6. If Cause is in the effect, and vice versa, how do we change effects?

7. When we "import rags and relics into the new hour," what is the effect in our experience?

8. What major paradigm have you replaced with a broader perspective?

9. "Nothing great was ever achieved without enthusiasm." Do you agree? Why is this so?

10. What is the difference between talents and character to Emerson?

RALPH WALDO EMERSON (1803–1882) was a renowned
lecturer and writer whose ideas on philosophy, religion,
and literature influenced many writers, including
Henry David Thoreau and Walt Whitman. After
an undergraduate career at Harvard, he studied at
Harvard Divinity School and became an ordained
minister, continuing the long line of ministers in his
family. He traveled widely and lectured, and became
well known for his publications *Nature* and *Essays*.

Dr. Carol Carnes has a varied background in
service and Global Ministry. Her career has spanned
three decades and has taken her around the world.
In the company of some of the great minds on the
planet—scientists, religious leaders, and cultural
icons—she has participated in three Synthesis
Dialogues with HH the Dalai Lama and other world
leaders in Italy and India. She helped plan the 2014
Awakened World Film Festival in Santa Barbara, the
Gandhi King Peace Train, and several New Thought
conferences. Her service to the international Centers
for Spiritual Living included serving as the Director
of Education and Member of the Board of Directors.
She was honored with a Doctor of Religious Science
award in 2010. Morehouse College, the alma mater

of Dr. Martin Luther King Jr., inducted her into the MLK International Board of Preachers in 2000. She has spoken at two of the Parliament of the World's Religions, in Cape Town, South Africa, and Melbourne, Australia.

She has written for *Creative Thought* and *Science of Mind* magazines and is the author of two previous books. Her daily blog "Living Consciously" serves as inspiration for thousands of people around the world. You can receive "Living Consciously" by subscribing via her website: **www.carol-carnes.com**

In her own words: "I believe the world is awakening to its spiritual roots, relieving itself of the superstition and dogma of Religion. To be spiritual is a way of living and thinking, not an institutionalized set of rules and regulations to follow. Spirituality ought to set us free to be authentically who we are and fully present wherever we are. Learning to honor and respect the creative nature of our own mind, seeing how we are one with the universal intelligence, can change lives dramatically. From physical healings to financial prosperity and all manner of healthy relationships, we can direct our own destiny with the right use of mind."